Chasing the Dragon

Assessing China's System of Export Controls for WMD-Related Goods and Technologies

Evan S. Medeiros

NATIONAL SECURITY RESEARCH DIVISION

The research described in this report was conducted within the RAND National Security Research Division, which conducts research and analysis for the Office of the Secretary of Defense, the Joint Staff, the Unified Commands, the defense agencies, the Department of the Navy, the U.S. intelligence community, allied foreign governments, and foundations.

Library of Congress Cataloging-in-Publication Data

Medeiros, Evan S.
    Chasing the dragon : assessing China's system of export controls for WMD-related goods and technologies / Evan S. Medeiros.
        p. cm.
    "MG-353."
    Includes bibliographical references.
    ISBN 0-8330-3805-2 (pbk. : alk. paper)
    1. Export controls—China. 2. Weapons of mass destruction—Government policy—China. 3. Arms transfers—China. I. Title.

HF1414.55.C6M43 2005
382'.64'0951—dc22

2005015780

The RAND Corporation is a nonprofit research organization providing objective analysis and effective solutions that address the challenges facing the public and private sectors around the world. RAND's publications do not necessarily reflect the opinions of its research clients and sponsors.

RAND® is a registered trademark.

Cover photo by Zhang Heping. Reproduced by permission from Imaginechina.

Published 2005 by the RAND Corporation
1776 Main Street, P.O. Box 2138, Santa Monica, CA 90407-2138
1200 South Hayes Street, Arlington, VA 22202-5050
201 North Craig Street, Suite 202, Pittsburgh, PA 15213-1516
RAND URL: http://www.rand.org/
To order RAND documents or to obtain additional information, contact
Distribution Services: Telephone: (310) 451-7002;
Fax: (310) 451-6915; Email: order@rand.org

Preface

This monograph examines the structure and operation of the Chinese government's evolving system of controls on exports of sensitive equipment, materials, and technologies that could be used in the production of weapons of mass destruction (WMD) and related delivery systems. The author identifies the key organizations involved in export control decisionmaking, the laws and regulations that form the basis of the government's system of controls, and the interactions among government organizations involved in vetting sensitive exports. This study assesses the strengths and weaknesses of this system's ability to implement and enforce government export controls and highlights areas that deserve more attention from Chinese policymakers.

As China emerges as a major power in the current global system, Beijing's national capacity to implement its multilateral security, trade, and other commitments directly informs U.S. and international assessments of China's ability to be a responsible major power as well as an effective administrator of its own economy and the party-state system. These issues are directly relevant to U.S. policymakers and scholars of both Chinese security affairs and international nonproliferation regimes.

This research was conducted within the Intelligence Policy Center of the RAND National Security Research Division (NSRD). NSRD conducts research and analysis for the Office of the Secretary of Defense, the Joint Staff, the Unified Commands, the defense agencies, the Department of the Navy, the U.S. intelligence community, allied foreign governments, and foundations.

For more information on the RAND Intelligence Policy Center, contact the Center's director, John Parachini. He can be reached by e-mail at john_parachini@rand.org; by phone at (703) 413-1100, extension 5579; or by mail at the RAND Corporation, 1200 S. Hayes Street, Arlington, VA 22202. More information about RAND is available at www.rand.org.

Contents

APPENDIX

Figures

Summary

The Chinese government's system of export controls on sensitive equipment, materials, and technologies used to produce weapons of mass destruction (WMD) and WMD delivery systems has undergone a significant evolution in the past 25 years. Chinese export controls have evolved since the early 1980s from highly underdeveloped and ineffective administrative procedures to a comprehensive collection of laws, regulations, circulars, and measures that incorporate the prevailing standards for international export control. The central government in recent years has also made efforts to improve interagency coordination on export control decisions. However, the Chinese government's inability to *consistently* and *effectively* implement and enforce these new controls is a persistent and glaring weakness of the current system. Further improvements will be gradual, and mixed, unless the Chinese government devotes more resources and political capital to bolstering its export control practices. Such an effort serves as a key indicator of the government's ability to fulfill its stated goal of acting like a "responsible major power" in global affairs, especially as related to WMD nonproliferation.

The Evolution of China's Export Control System

In the early 1980s, as China began to emerge as an active trading nation, its controls on sensitive WMD-related exports were extraordinarily weak and, in many instances, nonexistent. At the same time, the incentives to export such items, especially nuclear and missile goods, were substantial and growing. Until the mid-1990s, many controls were merely internal procedures that were opaque to foreigners and Chinese alike. The government used only administrative export controls that were a legacy of China's planned economy. (A similar system of "planned export" solely by state-designated entities also functioned in the Soviet Union until its collapse in 1991.)

China's system of weak and ineffective administrative controls began to change in the late 1980s and early 1990s as the government came under international pressure to better regulate exports of conventional military and WMD-related goods and technology to potential proliferators, especially in the Middle East and South Asia. During the latter half of the 1990s, Chinese leaders also began to recognize the negative impact on China's international image of being a supplier of WMD-related goods and technologies.

In response, China began transitioning to a system of legally based export controls in the mid-1990s. The government began promulgating laws, regulations, and measures that outlined government procedures for internally vetting pending exports of sensitive nuclear, chemical, missile, and conventional military goods and related technologies.

The evolution of China's controls on sensitive exports can be understood through the following evolutionary process, which occurred in nine overlapping stages: (1) limited internal/administrative controls and government policies that rhetorically supported *proliferation* as a tool of statecraft; (2) limited internal/administrative controls applied to some military-specific goods and government support for *nonproliferation*; (3) growing internal/administrative controls bolstered by narrow interministerial consultations and very limited high-level oversight of arms and WMD-related exports; (4) public, legally based export controls on conventional weapons and some nuclear and chemical weapons–related items; (5) public, legally based controls on *dual-use* nuclear and chemical items; (6) adoption and incorporation of international *control lists* (lists of materials, equipment, and technologies that are controlled under specific regulations) into existing regulations; (7) public and explicit controls on dual-use missile/aerospace and biological weapons–related goods; (8) full disclosure of the structure of the export control decisionmaking process and the policy standards used in decisionmaking; and (9) establishment of additional bureaucratic structures to implement and enforce existing export controls.

Several factors influenced the evolution of China's system of WMD export controls. First, the more specific an international treaty is about requiring export controls, the more responsive China has been in adopting explicit export control regulations related to that commitment. Second, bureaucratic weaknesses in implementing WMD-related export controls hampered the evolution of the system; in the 1980s, the government was not organized to make such decisions, and it took years to develop such institutional capabilities. Third, international pressure, mainly from the United States, played an important role in shaping China's policies on export regulation of sensitive goods and technologies. Lastly, changing Chinese views about the contributions of nonproliferation to Chinese foreign policy and national security interests were additional factors that influenced the evolution of China's export control system. These considerations, to vary degrees, continue to shape Chinese policymaking on WMD nonproliferation and export controls.

Structure of China's Export Control System

China has established a nascent but extensive interagency system to vet applications of sensitive exports. Several key government ministries actively participate in government decisions about licensing sensitive exports. The top-tier players in the process include the Ministry of Commerce (MOFCOM), the Ministry of Foreign Affairs (MFA); the General Administration of Customs (GAC); the China Atomic Energy Agency (CAEA); the CWC Implementation Office (CWCIO); the Commission on Science, Technology, and Industry for National Defense (COSTIND); the Ministry of Public Security/ Public Security Bureau (MPS/PSB); and, in some cases, the General Armaments Department (GAD) of the People's Liberation Army

(PLA). High-level offices in the State Council and the Central Military Commission can play a role in controversial decisions about particularly sensitive exports. Provincial bureaus of these agencies are also active in some aspects of export control administration.

Within the Chinese bureaucracy, there is also a host of secondary actors that contribute to export control administration, education, implementation, and enforcement. They include both government and nominally nongovernmental organizations, such as industry associations, government research institutes, think tanks, and major universities.

As a result of its efforts to reform its export control system, China has gradually created over the years a law-based "system" for controlling exports of WMD-related goods and technologies. The evolution of this system involved issuing laws, regulations, measures, circulars, and notices that collectively codified China's policy statements regarding nonproliferation. Another key step in creating this system involved incorporating various international standards for nonproliferation export control, such as erecting a registration and licensing system for sensitive exports, control lists, end-user and end-use certifications, "catch-all" principles (See Chapter Four), customs supervision, and punishments and penalties for violators of export control regulations. These elements are now part and parcel of the government's system of nonproliferation export controls.

In the past five years, China has promulgated regulations and measures covering exports of nuclear and nuclear dual-use goods, chemical-weapon and related dual-use items, conventional military products, dual-use biological goods and related technologies, and dual-use missile items. Detailed control lists of sensitive goods and technologies are part of each of these regulations; for example, the nuclear regulations incorporate international control lists developed by the Nuclear Suppliers Group (NSG).

Implementation and Enforcement of Export Controls

China's implementation and enforcement of its nonproliferation export controls serve as a key indicator of Beijing's willingness and ability to fulfill its nonproliferation pledges. This report treats these two issues somewhat differently. *Implementation* represents China's effort to translate government policy into practical actions within the Chinese government and between government and industry. *Enforcement* represents efforts by the Chinese to monitor the behavior of government entities and private companies, to identify violations by these entities and companies and, most important, to hold these organizations accountable for violating government rules and regulations.

In general terms, China has made far more substantial strides toward furthering implementation of controls than toward enforcement, although continued improvements in both areas are needed.

The Chinese government has taken several steps in recent years to improve implementation of WMD export controls. The first step, which is now largely complete, was the creation of a system of laws and regulations, as described above. Second, the government has established a process of formal interagency coordination to vet possible exports of WMD-related goods and technologies. Third, since late 2003, the government has identified detailed policy standards that are used in determining whether to license a sensitive export. Fourth, China has also developed an internal "watch list" of Chinese and foreign enterprises to monitor. Finally, Beijing is trying to enforce end-use/end-user controls, albeit with limited success. Even with these steps, much more effort is needed to further the implementation and enforcement of export control.

More specifically, a critical step in boosting implementation has been the Chinese government's efforts to inform, educate, and train both government officials and Chinese businessmen about their export control obligations. Numerous national- and provincial-level seminars have been conducted to educate Chinese industry officials about those obligations. The Chinese government has also begun to use the Internet to disseminate new rules and regulations and to facilitate the license application process for sensitive goods. Nevertheless, more education and training is needed.

The government faces numerous limitations in its ability to manage various export control processes. The main ones are limited financial resources and a lack of qualified people with adequate training expertise. These limitations suggest a lack of political will by the leadership to seriously implement nonproliferation export controls. In addition, MOFCOM does not have a computerized database of past and current export licenses (applied, denied, or approved) or of end users and end uses in various countries. The Chinese Customs Agency faces similar shortcomings. These limitations hinder the government's ability to verify end users or end uses, leaving gaps in the compliance system.

China's limited enforcement of its export controls is by far the weakest link in the export control system. The government's ability to detect, catch, investigate, and penalize export control violators is significantly underdeveloped. Critical gaps exist in many aspects of export control enforcement, especially monitoring, interdiction, and penalization. To be sure, these capabilities are better than they were a few years ago, but much more work needs to be done.

Several important points about the deficiencies in export control enforcement should be noted:

- It is not clear the extent to which this weakness results from a lack of political will to conduct hard-hitting investigations, a lack of resources, or both.
- China currently seems to rely largely on intelligence from foreign governments to learn about pending exports of illicit WMD-related goods and technologies. In many cases when the Chinese government has interdicted illegal WMD-related exports, Chinese officials have relied on intelligence data from the United States, the United Kingdom, and other nations.
- Continuing weaknesses in China's ability to investigate export control violations include MOFCOM and MPS's lack of experience in this area. In particular, their attitude in approaching such investigations shows a weakness in their investigative capa-

bilities. Their approach is often reactive, relying on the provision of Western intelligence data. In addition, there is a lack of healthy skepticism of Chinese firms that is needed to effectively conduct such investigations. MOFCOM officials also appear be unwilling to pursue investigations against large and influential Chinese state-owned enterprises.

As of April 2005, only two cases of government penalization for export control violations have been made public, but Chinese officials have stated that more are in the pipeline, including criminal cases that hold more severe penalties. There is no indication when such cases will come to fruition and/or be publicized.

Future Challenges for Chinese Export Controls

China is still several costly and time-consuming steps away from possessing a fully functioning export control system that can regularly monitor and police the activities of exporters involved in selling WMD-related goods and technologies. More resources need to be devoted to institutional development and defeating entrenched interests. Specifically, the Chinese government currently faces several challenges in erecting such a system:

- The need to regularize implementation of existing rules
- The need to significantly boost enforcement of export regulations and to communicate the cost of export control violations to state-owned and private enterprises
- The need to create incentives for better compliance by Chinese enterprises and, ultimately, to facilitate self-regulation by those enterprises
- The complexities posed by government reorganizations, which are common and often result in structural changes in the export control decisionmaking system

- The impact of the entry of China into the World Trade Organization and the resulting proliferation about Chinese companies with international trading rights
- The challenges posed by rapid enterprise privatization and the need to educate new companies about their nonproliferation obligations
- The growing foreign penetration into China's market and the increased opportunities for foreign enterprises to procure controlled items by exploiting the weaknesses in China's current export control system.

Acknowledgments

The author would like to thank Eric Valko for his extensive research assistance and for his help in drafting charts used in this report. I would also like to thank James Mulvenon and Scot Tanner for reading various drafts of this report and providing useful inputs. Michael Chase and Harlan Jencks deserve much gratitude for formally reviewing the entire manuscript and for suggesting important changes in nuance and substance. Heather Roy and Abigail Chapman provided assistance in organizing the travel for this study and for assistance in formatting a previous version of this document. I am particularly indebted to the numerous Chinese and Western officials, businesspeople, and analysts who shared their time and information during interviews conducted in China and the United States. Any and all mistakes are, of course, my own.

Acronyms

AG	Australia Group
BIS	U.S. Commerce Department Bureau of Industry and Security
BWC	Biological Weapons Convention
CACDA	China Arms Control and Disarmament Association
CANDU	Canadian Deuterium Uranium (Reactor)
CAEA	China Atomic Energy Agency
CASS	Chinese Academy of Social Sciences
CCCA	China Controlled Chemicals Association
CICIR	China Institute of Contemporary International Relations
CMC	Central Military Commission
CNEIC	China Nuclear Export-Import Corporation
COSTIND	Commission on Science, Technology, and Industry for National Defense
CW	chemical weapons
CWC	Chemical Weapons Convention
CWCIO	Chemical Weapons Convention Implementation Office
CZEC	China Zhongyuan Export Corporation

EU	European Union
FYP	Five-Year Plan
GAC	General Administration of Customs
GAD	General Armaments Department of the PLA
HS	harmonized system
IAEA	International Atomic Energy Agency
MFA	Ministry of Foreign Affairs
MOFCOM	Ministry of Commerce
MPS	Ministry of Public Security
MSS	Ministry of State Security
MTCR	Missile Technology Control Regime
NGO	nongovernmental organization
NPT	Treaty on the Nonproliferation of Nuclear Weapons
NSG	Nuclear Suppliers Group
OPCW	Organization for the Prohibition of Chemical Weapons
PLA	People's Liberation Army
PLC	pre-license check
PRC	People's Republic of China
PSB	Public Security Bureau
PSV	post-shipment verification
PUNT	Peaceful Uses of Nuclear Technology
SOE	state-owned enterprise
S&T	science and technology
TBP	tributyl phosphate
UN	United Nations
WMD	weapons of mass destruction
WTO	World Trade Organization

CHAPTER ONE

Introduction

Objective

As China becomes more integrated into the prevailing systems of rules, norms, and institutions on international security affairs, its ability (and willingness) to comply with its nonproliferation commitments will be an important indicator of the type of global actor that China will become in the future. This report addresses the broad issue of the Chinese government's institutional and administrative capacity to fulfill its international security commitments. Two broad questions motivated this research: Does the government possess the institutional structures and incentives to implement effectively its various economic and security commitments and, where deficiencies exist, does the government have the capacity to remedy them?

This report approaches these broad questions by examining the structure and operation of the Chinese government's system of controls on exports of sensitive equipment, materials, and technologies that could be used in the production of weapons of mass destruction (WMD) and related delivery systems.[1] China's export control system has consistently been a critical variable in understanding China's weapons proliferation behavior. The effectiveness of Beijing's export controls (in all forms) directly affects the government's ability to carry

---

[1] This study defines WMD-related equipment, materials, and technologies as those items included on the control lists of the Nuclear Suppliers Group (NSG), the Chemical Weapons Convention (CWC), the Biological Weapons Convention (BWC), and the Missile Technology Control Regime (MTCR).

out, fully and comprehensively, its political commitments under various multilateral and bilateral nonproliferation treaties and agreements. For many U.S. policymakers, China's official controls serve as the central indicator of the government's willingness to get serious about preventing WMD proliferation. Since the late 1990s, China has gradually improved its ability to control exports of WMD-related goods and technologies, but notable gaps remain, which raise questions about the degree of Beijing's commitment to nonproliferation.

In addition to the broad questions mentioned above, this report aims to answer several specific questions about China's export control system: How has China's export control system evolved since its inception? What factors have shaped this evolution? How is the current system structured? What is the legal basis of the system? Which government organizations play the most significant roles in this process? How does the system function, and does it work differently depending on the type of items being controlled? What types of policy guidelines do officials use in making export-licensing determinations? How effective is the government in implementing and enforcing controls? What are the major future challenges? How can the Chinese system be improved to bolster its controls on sensitive exports? While these questions are central to evaluating Chinese nonproliferation controls, they also inform our broader understanding of Chinese foreign policy, in particular the interrelationship between governance challenges and foreign policymaking.

Study Approach

This study relied heavily on four categories of information sources: (1) numerous interviews with Chinese government officials, analysts, and businesspeople who are directly and indirectly involved in China's export control decisionmaking process; (2) open-source Chinese-language materials, such as official laws, regulations, and circulars detailing the export control vetting process; (3) discussions with U.S. and Western diplomats and business people with knowledge of the structure and operation of China's export control system; and

(4) Western analysis of China's system of nonproliferation export controls. These categories of sources are collectively used, first, to erect a comprehensive picture of the structure and operation of China's export control system and, second, to evaluate its strengths and weaknesses.

Organization of This Report

Chapter Two provides an overview of the historical evolution of China's system of controls on sensitive exports, including during the pre-reform (pre-1978) period. Chapter Three describes the primary and secondary organizations involved in this system. Chapter Four examines the laws and regulations that constitute the backbone of the system; it also analyzes how the system vets possible exports of nuclear, chemical, missile, and conventional military-related items. Chapter Five addresses China's implementation and enforcement of its controls. Finally, Chapter Six outlines the key challenges to the effective functioning of the system in the coming years.

The appendices to this report contain copies of Chinese export control documents, including applications for the right to export sensitive goods and end-use and end-user applications. They were downloaded from Chinese government Web sites devoted to export control issues. For readers of Chinese,[2] these documents provide further details on China's nascent effort to build a modern and legally based export control system for WMD goods and technologies.

---

[2] Throughout this report, Chinese characters are included along with the *pinyin* Romanization of various terms to provide Chinese readers with more-precise descriptions of specific Chinese government organizations and concepts.

CHAPTER TWO

History of Chinese Export Controls

China's sales and transfers of sensitive goods used in the production of WMD and their delivery systems have long been issues of concern to the United States and the international community. In past decades, Chinese transfers of nuclear weapons–related and ballistic missile–related equipment, materials, and technologies have significantly aided the development of weapons programs in unstable regions of the world such as South Asia and the Middle East. While such assistance from China was extensive in the 1980s and early 1990s, it has narrowed since the mid-1990s. The Chinese government began to expand its formal participation in and adherence to key nonproliferation treaties and non-treaty–based supplier-control agreements. As its participation increased, China gradually began to formalize and institutionalize these policy positions by creating public, legally based regulations governing the export of sensitive goods controlled by various nonproliferation treaties and agreements.

The evolution of this system of formal export controls on sensitive WMD exports has been gradual. Its development has occurred in fits and starts and has often been linked to key diplomatic trends, such as shifts in U.S.-China political relations, U.S. demands for greater attention being paid by China to nonproliferation, and efforts by the Chinese to improve their own international image. Even as China erected this export control system, however, sensitive exports of chemical-weapon and missile-related items have continued. Thus, China's export control system can serve as an important indicator of the government's ability and willingness to carry out its various and growing nonproliferation commitments. From the vantage point of 2005, the government's export control system—on paper—appears to be extensive. China has not only promulgated numerous laws (*falu,* 法律), regulations (*tiaoli,* 条例), and measures (*banfa,* 办法), but has also incorporated into them international *control lists* (lists of materials, equipment, and technologies that are controlled under specific regulations), and key attributes of a modern export-control administration, such as "catch-all controls." The government has also publicly outlined the various policy standards it uses to evaluate pending exports of sensitive WMD and missile-related exports to countries all over the world.

Despite these reforms and improvements, the functioning of the existing system leaves much to be desired. Numerous weaknesses persist, and they allow for continued transfers of sensitive WMD-related items to potential proliferators.

As stated in Chapter One, the purpose of this report is to outline and analyze the current structure and operation of China's export control system for sensitive goods and technologies. The report assesses China's formal system of controls on sales of nuclear-, chemical-, and missile-related items. The government's ability to implement and enforce these laws and regulations has received much attention. As China accelerates the marketization of its economy and its integration into the international economy, the challenges to effective export-control enforcement will grow geometrically.

Historical Evolution of China's Export Controls

China's system of controls of sensitive, weapons-related exports has evolved significantly in the 55-plus years of the People's Republic of China (PRC).[1] Following the founding of the PRC in 1949, China's controls on military-related exports were essentially de facto controls

---

[1] For a good overview of the historical evolution of Chinese export controls, see Jonathan E. Davis, *Export Controls of the People's Republic of China 2005,* Athens Ga.: Center for International Trade and Security, University of Georgia, February 2005.

that were a function of three considerations: a centrally planned economy, an economic development strategy that stressed autarky over international trade, and a developing science and technology base that focused on developing military capabilities for China. It was not until the 1970s that China had developed nuclear and missile industries that were in a position to sell such critical technologies to other countries; even then, such goods were the crown jewels of China's defense industrial establishment and not likely to be exported. The planned nature of China's economy exerted the main influence on Chinese export behavior. The Chinese government in the pre-reform period heavily subsidized the operations of its critical defense industries, and thus such firms possessed minimal incentives to export their goods. In addition, under China's planned economy, the government specifically designated very few "trading" companies with the authority to conduct import-export activities. This right was tightly controlled, and other state-run companies simply did not have the opportunity to conduct such trade outside this tightly administered system of export-import controls.[2] This process of state-controlled and directed trade was outlined in a variety of laws and statutes that were adopted in the early 1950s when Mao's centrally planned economy was first being erected.[3]

China's weapons and military-related exports in the pre-reform period were largely driven by China's foreign policy goals and not economic considerations. In other words, these were state-directed transfers and were officially sanctioned. China transferred, often free of charge, weapons and military goods to a host of nations

[2] See Nicholas R. Lardy, *Foreign Trade and Economic Reform in China, 1978–1990*, Cambridge, UK: Cambridge University Press, 1992; Barry Naughton, *Growing Out of the Plan*, Cambridge, UK: Cambridge University Press, 1996.

[3] China's first trade statues were the December 1950 "Provisional Rules of Foreign Trade Administration (*Duiwai Maoyi Guanli Zanxing Tiaoli*) and a subsequent decree called "Detailed Rules Regarding the Provisional Rules of Foreign Trade Administration" (*Duiwai Maoyi Guanli Zanxing Tiaoli Shishi Xizhe*). These two statutes established a basic licensing system for the first few years of the PRC until the First Five-Year Plan (FYP) was created. Yet, once the government nationalized all industry in the mid-1950s, then all import-export activities were governed by a small number of state-owned trading companies.

in Africa and Southeast Asia that were part China's effort to fight "imperialism" and "revisionism." While China provided large quantities of conventional military goods to its friends and clients, it transferred very few WMD-related goods. Chinese leaders rhetorically opposed nuclear nonproliferation in this period but seemed to have stopped short of actually supporting and facilitating nuclear proliferation. Beijing reportedly refused requests from both Egypt and Libya for nuclear weapons assistance.[4] That said, China during the pre-reform period did conduct some WMD-related exports. China transferred a few rudimentary ballistic missiles to North Korea in the mid-1970s, but the assistance stopped a few years later. North Korea's subsequent development of ballistic missiles in the 1990s appears have limited technical lineage to Chinese missile technologies.[5] In addition, one of the most curious WMD exports during this period was China's transfer of numerous chemical weapons (CW) to Albania in the mid-1970s. Very little is known about the origins, motivations, or mechanisms of this particular deal, which was only discovered by Albanian officials in 2004.[6] China's most notorious transfer to Pakistan of nuclear weapons design, materials, and related technologies did not occur until the early 1980s. This case was not an export control problem but rather a specific policy decision, presumably made by China's most senior leaders.[7]

---

[4] Mohamed Heikal, *The Cairo Documents*, New York, N.Y.: Doubleday Press, 1973; Shyman Bhatia, *Nuclear Rivals in the Middle East*, New York, N.Y.: Routledge Press, 1988, p. 56, 59, 66; "Will China Assume a New Responsibility?" *Washington Post*, November 22, 1971, p. A20.

[5] John Wilson Lewis and Hua Di, "China's Ballistic Missile Programs: Technologies Strategies and Goals," *International Security,* Fall 1992, pp. 5-40. On North Korea's missile programs, see David Wright, *Assessment of the North Korean Missile Threat*, Cambridge, Mass.: Union of Concerned Scientists, February 2003 (www.ucsusa.org).

[6] Joby Warrick, "Albania's Chemical Cache Raises Fears About Others, Long-Forgotten Arms Had Little or No Security," *Washington Post*, January 10, 2005, p. A01.

[7] The design provided to Pakistan was based on China's fourth nuclear weapons test, which China conducted on October 27, 1966. "The Pakistani Nuclear Program," June 23, 1983, US Department of State, Bureau of Intelligence and Research, declassified and released under the Freedom of Information Act to the National Security Archive (Washington, DC), January 17, 1991.

Reform Era Creates New Challenges

China's controls on exports of WMD goods and technologies faced a number of new challenges in the early 1980s as China began to trade and engage with the international community. As the era of "reform and openness" began, China's controls were highly underdeveloped and inadequate in the face of emerging pressures to export. The incentives for Chinese state-owned companies to export such items were substantial and growing. As Deng Xiaoping initiated the "reform and openness" policy, China was in the historically unusual position of being a poor, developing country that also possessed large and, in some cases, geographically dispersed nuclear, aerospace, and petrochemical industries. China's nuclear and aerospace industries had been heavily oriented toward military production since their inception. Yet, under Deng's reforms, they were mandated to generate much of their own funding to reduce the burden on the state. This situation created incentives to export nuclear and aerospace products to keep factories open, production lines running, and, most important, people employed. As a result, throughout the 1980s, Chinese nuclear and aerospace industry firms began to sell significant amounts of sensitive nuclear and missile goods to aspiring proliferators all over the world.

Furthermore, government controls on sensitive exports were as weak as the financial motives for Chinese companies were strong. China participated in none of the major international nonproliferation treaties and agreements. Chinese leaders, especially the aging revolutionary guard, were highly skeptical of such accords, viewing them as inherently discriminatory and as a means for the "superpowers" to constrain China's economic development and foreign policy goals. Indeed, for most political, military, and business leaders, economic development was China's chief imperative, while nonprolifera-

Also see Leslie Gelb, "Peking Said to Balk at Nuclear Pledges," *New York Times*, June 23, 1984, p. 3. The projected size of China's fourth test was 12–30 kilotons. It was a fission device. China tested the device on a DF-2 (CSS-1) missile. For details on Chinese nuclear tests, see Robert S. Norris et al., *Chinese, French, and British Nuclear Weapons, Nuclear Weapons Databook*, Vol. 5, Washington, D.C.: Natural Resources Defense Council, 1995.

tion was seen as the "rich-man's burden." One of the most glaring examples of the weaknesses of Chinese controls occurred in 1982 when a Chinese shipment of un-safeguarded heavy water (D_2O, which is used as a coolant in nuclear reactors) was sold, via an international broker, to India for use in its nuclear weapons program. New Delhi, which had been searching for years for a source of un-safeguarded heavy water for its Canadian CANDU reactors, found an unwitting supplier in China, its main regional adversary.[8]

Even when China issued its first policy statements about nuclear nonproliferation in the mid-1980s, it was unclear whether the government understood how to carry out these pledges and whether internal controls existed to implement such pledges. For example, when China joined the International Atomic Energy Agency (IAEA) in 1984, it pledged to (1) place all of its exports under IAEA safeguards, (2) not assist nuclear weapons programs, and (3) not re-transfer Chinese nuclear goods without government consent. While this pledge stopped China's most egregious exports of un-safeguarded nuclear material to nuclear weapons programs in South Africa, Argentina, Brazil, and India, this pledge did not stop China's nuclear exports to Iran, Pakistan, or Algeria. By 1987, China adopted its first *Regulations on the Control of Nuclear Materials*, which created controls on exports of sensitive nuclear *materials,* such as enriched uranium and plutonium. This initial regulation, however, did not address exports of nuclear equipment or related nuclear technologies.[9]

Until the mid-1990s, China's controls on exports of WMD goods and technologies were either nonexistent or were internal procedures that were opaque to the international community.[10] There was no formal licensing system based on government laws and regulations. Chinese diplomats were very reluctant to share details about

---

[8] Leonard S. Spector, *Nuclear Proliferation Today*, New York, N.Y.: Vintage Books, 1984, pp. 318–319.

[9] See Weixing Hu, "China's Nuclear Export Controls: Policy and Regulations," *The Nonproliferation Review*, Vol. 1, No. 2, Winter 1994.

[10] The one exception to this was the *Regulations on Control of Nuclear Materials* issued in 1987, which was initially an internal document.

their export decisions with their counterparts in other countries, adding to the skepticism about the effectiveness of Chinese controls.[11] At that time, these internal controls could only loosely be called a "system." The government used the old system of "administrative" controls, which contrasts with the current system of "legally based" export controls. Such administrative controls were a legacy of China's planned economy; a similar system of "planned exports" functioned in the Soviet Union/Russia in the 1980s and 1990s.

The system of "administrative controls" had several features. First, all controls were internal executive decrees, not public documents and not grounded in Chinese law.[12] Second, under this system, the State Council had designated certain state-owned trading firms as the only entities permitted to export sensitive items. This was especially true for exports of nuclear, missile, and conventional military items that were sold by state-controlled entities. This monopoly of trading rights provided the government with a degree of control over who exported sensitive items, what was exported, and who received them. Yet, there were also extensive problems with this system, given the penchant for companies to ignore or circumvent these stipulations due to the Chinese government's broader political agenda of promoting economic development and trade.

A third attribute of these administrative controls was the centralized control of export decisions within one industrial bureaucracy (e.g., the nuclear industry). For many years, there was little, if any, *interministerial* coordination or vetting process. In the 1980s, the Ministry of Nuclear Industry (which became the China National Nuclear Corporation in 1993) made decisions about nuclear exports by its trading firms, for example. These decisions were made each year according to the yearly plan, which operated in conjunction with the industry's five-year planning cycle. This nascent system of export

---

[11] Interviews with U.S. officials involved in U.S.-China export control negotiations, Washington, D.C., 2004.

[12] Fu Cong, "An Introduction of China's Export Control System," Department of Arms Control and Disarmament, Ministry of Foreign Affairs of China, statement at Workshop on Nonproliferation Export Control Regimes, Tokyo, December 11–12, 1997.

oversight by industry leaders, as one would expect, created incentives for exporting and *not* for limiting sales of sensitive items. Even though the Ministry of Nuclear Industry in the 1980s was China's chief point of contact for IAEA affairs in Vienna, it viewed exports as its political prerogative and as a source of needed hard currency. The IAEA norm of responsible nuclear exporting took years to seep into the nuclear industry bureaucracy. Similarly, military-run companies (*jundui qiye,* 军队企业) and defense industrial firms (*jungong qiye,* 军工企业) controlled decisions about exports of conventional weapons from the military's stockpiles or from defense factory production lines.[13]

This system of monopolistic administrative export control authority began to change in the late 1980s and early 1990s as the government received international pressure to bolster controls on sensitive exports to potential proliferants, especially in the Middle East and South Asia. Key industrial firms in the nuclear and aerospace industries began to consult with government agencies, such as the Ministry of Foreign Affairs (MFA, 外交部) about pending sales so the latter could provide an impact assessment for China's foreign policy.[14] In the late 1980s, a leading high-level group under the State Council and Central Military Commission was established to vet sensitive military exports. The creation of this organ did not guarantee substantial limits on such behavior, however. The MFA was seldom the strongest bureaucratic actor in such internal deliberations. In addition, as mentioned above, senior Chinese leaders at that time continued to view trade and economic development as a national im-

---

[13] China's defense industrial enterprises (*jungong qiye*) are state-owned industries that produce weapons and equipment for China's military; they are distinct from "military enterprises" (*jundui qiye*), which used to be owned and operated by the People's Liberation Army (PLA) until divestiture by the PLA in the late 1990s. In July 1999, Jiang Zemin called for the PLA to sever its ties to all business enterprises. This process is ongoing. See James C. Mulvenon, *Chinese Military Commerce and U.S. National Security*, Santa Monica, Calif.: RAND Corporation, 1997.

[14] Lu Ning, *The Dynamics of Foreign-Policy Decisionmaking in China*, Boulder, Colo.: Westview Press, 1997, p. 143–144.

perative and were equally skeptical of (and sometimes outwardly hostile toward) certain international nonproliferation accords.

There were two other weaknesses in China's system of administrative controls on sensitive exports. First, China did not issue any public control lists, claiming to use internal ones. But it was never clear which equipment, materials, and technologies were included on these internal lists, or if they even existed. During U.S.-China negotiations on nonproliferation in the 1990s, U.S. diplomats frequently asked China about the scope of internal controls on nuclear and missile items. On several occasions in the mid-1990s, Chinese diplomats affirmed the existence of such lists but refused to produce them. One of the most glaring gaps in these control lists was the apparent lack of coverage of *dual-use goods* (goods and technology developed for civilian use that can also be used for military applications or to produce WMD). A final failing of such administrative controls was the absence of clear policy standards to judge whether to export sensitive items to certain countries. Financial incentives appeared to be the strongest motive in decisionmaking, and it was not until the early 1990s that China began to consider the impact of these sales on its international image.

Transition from Administrative to Legally Based Controls on Sensitive Exports

China began to transition from a system of administrative controls to a system of legally based export controls in the mid-1990s. In 1994, China adopted a general and comprehensive Foreign Trade Law, which outlined, for the first time, the legal parameters of all foreign trade in China—including general export controls. In 1987, China adopted its first Customs Law, which empowered the Customs Agency to participate in vetting exports.[15] With these laws as the legal basis and government nonproliferation pledges as a political basis

---

[15] The original 1987 Customs Law was subsequently revised in 2000.

for export controls, the government then began issuing regulations governing the sales of sensitive chemical, nuclear, and military items. These and other regulations also explicitly addressed the export of sensitive *dual-use* items in these same categories. The last step was an important one for China, as exports of sensitive dual-use items had become an issue in China's foreign relations. In subsequent years, the scope of controls expanded. Regulations governing controls on missile-related and biological weapons–related goods gradually emerged. All of these regulations will be analyzed in greater detail in later chapters of this report.

The evolution of China's controls on sensitive exports can be understood according to the following sequence. The process oc-curred in nine stages from the early 1980s to today.

1. Limited internal/administrative controls and government policies supporting proliferation
2. Limited internal/administrative controls applied to some general types of military-specific goods and government support for non-proliferation
3. Growing internal/administrative controls bolstered by narrow interministerial consultations and very limited high-level oversight
4. Public, legally based export controls on conventional weapons and some nuclear and chemical weapons–related items
5. Public, legally based controls on *dual-use* nuclear and chemical items
6. Adoption and incorporation of international control lists into ex-isting regulations
7. Public and explicit controls on dual-use missile/aerospace–related and biological weapons–related goods
8. Full disclosure of the structure of the export control decisionmak-ing system and the policy standards used in decisionmaking
9. Establishment of additional bureaucratic structures to implement and enforce existing controls.

Several factors related to China's understanding of nonprolifera-tion affairs and its foreign relations influenced the evolution and improvement of China's system of controls on sensitive exports. First, the nature and scope of China's treaty commitments have shaped China's attitude toward export controls. The more specific a treaty is about requiring export controls, the more responsive China has been in adopting explicit export control regulations. When a nonproliferation treaty is vague about specifying export control requirements (such as the requirements of the Treaty on the Nonproliferation of Nuclear Weapons [NPT]), China was slow to establish rigorous export controls on sensitive goods (such those covering nuclear technologies or dual-use nuclear goods). This pattern of behavior is most evident when one compares China's policies on controlling sensitive nuclear and chemical-weapon exports. The Chemical Weapons Convention treaty calls for all signatories to put into place rigorous and comprehensive export control regulations on CWC-controlled items listed in the treaty's "schedules" of such items. China signed the CWC in 1993 and ratified it in April 1997. The CWC's explicit and detailed export control obligations prompted China to issue its first two regulations on sensitive CW-related exports to facilitate ratification of the treaty. In December 1995, China adopted the "Regulations on Controlled Chemicals," which governed exports of all CWC-controlled items. In March 1997, China adopted a supplement to the 1995 regulations to further outline the regulations' implementation details. This supplement was needed to address some of the weak language in the original 1995 regulations, which were vague and broad in parts. This supplement also allowed China to move forward with CWC ratification later that year. Following the promulgation of the 1995 and 1997 export control regulations and other related steps on export controls,[16] the National People's Congress

---

[16] As part of its CWC obligations, China declared the existence of small-scale facilities for the production of chemical weapon agents. China claims to have destroyed all these facilities. China also declared that it maintains a defensive chemical warfare program to protect itself against chemical attack, which is not in conflict with the CWC. The Organization for the Prohibition of Chemical Weapons (OPCW) has conducted several inspections in China to verify the veracity of China's statements.

then ratified the CWC and submitted to the Organization for the Prohibition of Chemical Weapons (OPCW) its instrument of ratification in April 1997.

A second factor influencing the evolution of this system was China's weaknesses in implementing these types of controls; the government was not organized to effectively administer export controls, and it took time to adjust. China's approach to nuclear nonproliferation controls serves as a prominent example of these challenges. Although China joined the NPT in 1992, it took few steps to institutionalize NPT commitments into formal and public export controls. For years before *and* after China's ratification of the NPT in 1992, the Chinese government relied on internal *administrative* controls to govern nuclear sales abroad. Also, since the NPT (unlike the CWC) does not specifically require the issuance of export control regulations, the Chinese government did not pursue the step of issuing export control regulations as part of its ratification of the NPT.

In the mid-1990s, as the weaknesses in Chinese controls on nuclear exports became evident to officials, the government began to address those weaknesses by formalizing controls on sensitive nuclear exports. An international incident in spring 1996 surrounding the sale by a Chinese company of ring magnets to a Pakistani institute involved in the nuclear weapons program catalyzed the Chinese bureaucracy to move toward formal and comprehensive nuclear export control regulations.[17] The sale of these ring magnets highlighted to Chinese officials the need to establish comprehensive and public export controls on nuclear-specific and nuclear dual-use items. Based on the author's discussions with Chinese officials, the ring-magnet incident uniquely highlighted to those officials the weaknesses and inadequacies of China's "internal control system" and the corresponding need for controls based on international standards and in-

---

As mentioned earlier, in the mid-1970s, China reportedly transferred a large quantity of various CW agents to Albania, which was only recently discovered by the Albanian government. See Warrick, 2005, p. A01.

[17] The sale actually occurred in summer 1995, but it was not publicly revealed until spring 1996.

ternational control lists.[18] In 1997, a year after the ring-magnet incident and during the lead-up to a major summit meeting between the U.S. and Chinese presidents, China issued, initially, a circular on nuclear export controls in May 1997. In September 1997, China then issued its first public set of regulations governing exports of nuclear equipment and technologies.[19] A year later, in 1998, the State Council promulgated additional regulations governing dual-use nuclear items. Both sets of regulations used the controls lists of the NSG as their baseline.

International pressure, mainly from the United States, played an important role in shaping China's policies on export control regulation. The United States placed a high priority on nonproliferation in bilateral relations, and at specific times Washington pressed Beijing to formalize its nonproliferation policy commitments into specific export control regulations. At varying times in U.S.-China relations, the United States linked improvements in China's export control capabilities to improvements in U.S.-China relations. U.S. officials sought to identify for China specific problems with its existing controls (internal and public) and pressed Beijing to fix the leaks in the existing system. This approach resulted in numerous improvements in China's existing export controls.

The role of U.S. incentives and pressure on China to bolster its nonproliferation controls cut across a range of nonproliferation issues and resulted in efforts by the Chinese government to improve controls on nuclear, chemical, conventional military, and missile-related goods. Examples of these efforts abound. In 1997, China's promulgation of nuclear-specific export regulations was a specific precondition for the United States to move forward with implementation of a dormant 1985 bilateral nuclear cooperation agreement for peaceful

---

[18] This insight is based on the author's numerous discussions with Chinese and U.S. officials involved in this episode as well as Chinese analysts involved in nonproliferation policy-making. These interviews occurred in Beijing and Washington, from 2000 to 2004.

[19] According to a Chinese nonproliferation expert, the export control regulations were actually in effect since May 1997 when China issued a *circular* on controlling nuclear exports. The subsequent regulations were published in *People's Daily* and *Nuclear Industry News* to highlight their importance to U.S. policymakers.

uses of nuclear energy. During a 1998 summit meeting of the U.S. and Chinese presidents, China agreed to expand the list of controlled CW items to include ten chemicals that were included in the control list of the Australia Group (AG)—an organization that China criticized for years as a discriminatory, cartel-like agreement among global suppliers of CW-related goods and technologies. In addition, China's relative unwillingness for years to issue missile-related export control regulations was intimately tied to Chinese opposition U.S. arms sales to Taiwan. On this issue, U.S. pressure to issue such regulations had both a positive and negative influence, as China's behavior on missile proliferation became closely linked to the vicissitudes in U.S.-China relations. While China for years resisted issuing specific missile export controls, the government finally took this step in August 2002 to indicate the importance it placed on nonproliferation affairs, both globally and in U.S.-China relations. To this day, China's implementation and enforcement of certain export controls continue to be linked *to some degree* to the tenor and tone of U.S.-China political relations. This linkage has loosened significantly but remains an influence on Chinese policymaking in certain areas.[20]

Additional influences on the evolution of China's approach to nonproliferation and export controls have been the changes in Chinese views about the importance of nonproliferation to Chinese foreign policy and national security interests. As the beliefs of policymakers and analysts about the relative benefit of nonproliferation to Chinese economic and security interests have shifted, so has Beijing's willingness to improve its export control regulations. This view of the contribution of nonproliferation to Chinese interests has accelerated

---

[20] The link has loosened because Chinese leaders have recognized the dangers of WMD proliferation to China's growing global interests, particularly after September 11, 2001. Yet, the link persists for some Chinese policymakers because their perception is that the United States regularly asks China to go beyond its international nonproliferation commitments in meeting U.S. demands for halting certain types of exports to particular countries. Many Chinese also see the United States as using nonproliferation to push China to adopt Washington's foreign policy approach toward key regions.

since September 11, 2001, in particular.[21] China has been more active on nonproliferation issues (such as CW and nuclear nonproliferation) now that it generally accepts that such policies represent an international consensus (*guoji gongshi,* 国际共识) and serve Beijing's national security interests.[22] Indeed, today in China there is little internal debate about the contribution of CW and nuclear nonproliferation to Chinese national security.

As a result, China has taken successive steps to improve, on paper, its formal controls over nuclear and CW exports, even when such controls are unpopular among exporters and industrial conglomerates interested in expanding market share and profits. By contrast, controls on dual-use items addressed in supplier regimes such as the AG and the MTCR have historically been weaker within China; for years, Chinese officials commonly viewed such regimes as lacking an international mandate and not reflecting international standards. Such regimes were commonly reviled, even among Chinese nonproliferation specialists. The longstanding opposition to supplier regimes is clearly changing as Chinese officials articulate a growing interest in joining certain multilateral nonproliferation regimes and incorporating their controls into Chinese regulations. China's successful effort to join the Nuclear Suppliers Group in 2004 and its failed attempt to join the MTCR later that year are an indication of the shift in Chinese views of the value of such supplier-control regimes.

---

[21] Wu Xinbo, "The Promise and Limitations of Sino-US Partnership," *The Washington Quarterly*, Autumn 2004, pp. 115–126.

[22] This language was specifically used in a December 2003 white paper on nonproliferation (*China's Non-Proliferation Policy and Measures* [*Zhongguo Bukuosan Zhengce he Cuoshi,* 中国的防扩散政策和措施], Beijing, China: State Council Information Office, December 2003 (http://www.china.org.cn/e-white/20031202/index.htm; last accessed April 2004).

CHAPTER THREE

Key Organizations in China's Export Control System

Several government organizations are involved in vetting exports of WMD-related goods and technologies. The various bureaucratic actors and their respective roles and responsibilities are delineated in this chapter and are summarized and diagrammed in Figure 3.1. Understanding the bureaucratic "playing field" in China and the relative distribution of authority among these organizations is central to evaluating how the system functions and its future evolution.

Ministry of Commerce

China's Ministry of Commerce (MOFCOM, 商务部) is the lead organization in the Chinese bureaucracy tasked with export control administration for controlled WMD goods and technologies. As Chinese leaders have placed more emphasis on WMD nonproliferation in recent years, MOFCOM's export control responsibilities, resources, and authority have all grown. In one way or another, MOFCOM is involved in almost every decision regarding the licensing of exports of sensitive goods and technologies, except for conventional military goods.[1] While China has sought to strengthen its export control bureaucracy by establishing clearer lines of authority, it has also placed responsibility for export controls in the very

---

[1] The reason for this exception is explained later in this chapter.

Figure 3.1
China's Export Control System: National-Level Organizations

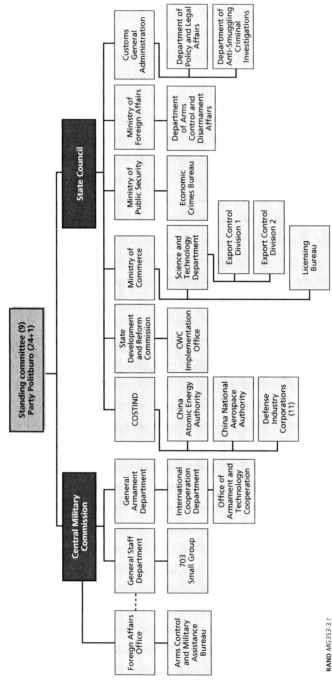

same government ministry that is also tasked with encouraging Chinese exports. MOFCOM's dual mandates could affect its decisionmaking, especially decisionmaking among more-senior MOFCOM officials who may not be familiar with the nuances of WMD export control administration.[2]

The majority of MOFCOM's export control issues are handled in the Department of Scientific and Technological Development and Trade (also known as the "Science and Technology Department" or *Kejisi* 科技司). MOFCOM also has a licensing bureau that is responsible for issuing export control licenses once policy decisions have been made; its role is strictly administrative.

Within this Science and Technology Department, there are two divisions (or *chu*, 处) tasked with handling export control issues; these two divisions were created from one division in 2003 due to the growing workload in each area. Division One (*Yi Chu*, 一处) is tasked with "outward" export control issues related to Chinese imports of foreign-controlled technologies, such as advanced machine tools. This division handles all pre-license checks (PLCs) and post-shipment verification (PSV) issues. A second, larger division handles Chinese controls on exports of sensitive items and, thus, is the main focus of this monograph. Division Two (*Er Chu*, 二处) has some eight to ten employees with varying levels of experience working on export control issues. The division's work is guided by senior members of the Science and Technology Department, who have far more experience than other department members and who have shown a willingness to devote attention and resources to WMD export control administration. This division also aspires to develop sector-by-sector expertise in the future. However, Division Two also suffers from limited expertise and resources. Many of its staffers are recent college graduates with limited interest and experience in export control administration. As noted later in this chapter, they are

---

[2] To be sure, a situation similar to this also exists in the U.S. Commerce Department. In China, it is not clear how much this tension plays out in actual export control decisionmaking.

responsible for a diverse range of multiple activities that are critical to effective export control administration.[3]

The Science and Technology Department's Division Two possesses several responsibilities critical to vetting exports of controlled items. Its main responsibilities are twofold:

1. It administers the processes by which Chinese companies (including joint ventures and wholly owned foreign enterprises) are, first, granted the right for general trading authority to export or import goods from or to China[4] and, second, granted permission to engage in exports of controlled sensitive items.[5] There are separate applications for granting these two rights. The certification process for granting the latter right is new in China, and permission is granted on a three-year, renewable basis. The latter right can be renewed, assuming that the company has not engaged in illicit activity and has not been subject to administrative or criminal penalties. These two types of certification are formally outlined in Chinese regulations.

2. MOFCOM is the lead government department in charge of reviewing applications for all potential exports of controlled *dual-use* nuclear, chemical, and missile equipment, materials, and technologies. MOFCOM coordinates the license application process and leads the interagency consultations on such applications. By contrast, MOFCOM is *not* the main point of contact for licensing decisions regarding major nuclear, chemical,[6] missile, or conven-

---

[3] By comparison, the Bureau of Industry and Security (BIS) in the U.S. Department of Commerce employs a few hundred personnel.

[4] Some 400,000 to 500,000 entities currently have such authority. Now that China is a member in the World Trade Organization (WTO), this step of requiring a government license to export will soon be abolished. Chinese companies granted business licenses will automatically be granted permission to export and import.

[5] MOFCOM states that some 150 to 200 companies currently have such authority. For more information on Chinese export controls, see www.mofcom.gov.cn (Chinese) or http://english.mofcom.gov.cn/ (English).

[6] There is one small exception to licensing of chemical exports. The licensing of exports of dual-use chemical goods is split between MOFCOM and China's CWC Implementation

tional military items. Principal responsibility for licensing such items resides in other government departments, which are specified later in this chapter. Even in those situations, MOFCOM participates in the interagency consultations for such license applications.

MOFCOM's authority extends to the critical areas of export control implementation and enforcement. MOFCOM officials in Beijing and provincial MOFCOM officials are directly involved in educating Chinese industry officials about China's export control regulations and the industries' responsibilities to abide by them. Various training seminars throughout China have been held in this regard, often in coordination with other government organizations, such as the Commission on Science, Technology, and Industry for National Defense (COSTIND). MOFCOM headquarters has organized two such training seminars jointly with the U.S. Department of Commence in 1998 and 2003 and held one with the European Union (EU) in January 2005. China's first nationwide export control seminar was held in February 2003, and additional provincial-level MOFCOM seminars on export controls have also been convened.

MOFCOM's authority also now extends to initiating and conducting investigations of illicit or unlicensed exports of controlled items. This is a relatively new authority for MOFCOM and is a reflection of its designation as the lead government agency in charge of export controls. As the Chinese government has increased its attention to nonproliferation in recent years, MOFCOM has been empowered by the State Council with a growing number of rights and responsibilities to implement the export control aspects of China's nonproliferation pledges.

Export control investigations can occur in several ways. MOFCOM can and has initiated rapid-reaction investigations to

---

Office. MOFCOM is responsible for licensing exports of all dual-use CWC-controlled items (items in the third schedule of the CWC) and the dual-use items added to the control list in fall 2002. The CWC Implementation Office has responsibility for licensing exports of the ten dual-use chemical items that were added to China's chemical control list in June 1998. These ten items are on the Australia Group's control list (see Chapter Two).

prevent exports of controlled items, often based on the provision of intelligence from foreign governments (mainly the United States and the United Kingdom).[7] These investigations are usually conducted in conjunction with Customs, the Ministry of Public Security (MPS), and the Foreign Ministry. In fact, several Chinese officials have stated that in 2004 China established a hotline and rapid response team to deal with urgent cases of impending exports of illicit items. These new capabilities have been used to prevent transfers of controlled goods to North Korea, for example. Drawing on its investigations, MOFCOM possesses the power to levy administrative fines against Chinese entities, depending on the nature of the infraction. In May 2004, MOFCOM publicly announced that administrative sanctions were imposed on two unnamed Chinese firms for missile technology exports.[8] If criminal intent is determined in a case of an unlicensed export, then MOFCOM can call for a criminal investigation, which is conducted by the MPS. For the past few years, Chinese officials have regularly stated that such investigations are currently underway, although there has been no evidence to date of a criminal conviction in an export control case.

---

[7] A recent and public example of investigation and interdiction involves the attempted export in summer 2003 of tributyl phosphate (TBP, which is used in reprocessing spent nuclear fuel to extract plutonium) to North Korea. Based on U.S. intelligence data, the Chinese interdicted the shipment. This incident was made public in a 2003 speech by then-Secretary of State Colin Powell. See "Remarks at Conference on China-U.S. Relations," Secretary of State Colin L. Lowell, Texas A&M University, College Station, Texas, November 5, 2003 (http://www.state.gov/secretary/former/powell/remarks/2003/25950. htm; last accessed April 12, 2005).

[8] See "Liang gongsi yin weifan chukou guanzhi de youguan guiding xingzheng chufa," "两公司因违反出口管制的有关规定遭行政处罚" (http://exportcontrol.mofcom.gov. cn/article/200408/20040800269548_1.xml; last accessed April 25, 2005); also see "Two Chinese Companies Fined for Violating Regulations on Missile Export Control," *People's Daily*, last updated May 26, 2004 (http://english.peopledaily.com.cn/200405/26/eng2004 0526_144379.html; last accessed April 12, 2005).

Ministry of Foreign Affairs

The MFA's Department of Arms Control and Disarmament Affairs (*Junkong Si*, 军控司) is also a central player in decisionmaking processes for vetting exports of controlled WMD goods; this is by virtue of its position as the chief interpreter of China's multilateral and bilateral nonproliferation commitments and the government agency tasked with assessing the potential impact of China's foreign relations. While this department is involved in all aspects of export control policymaking, its role has diminished to some extent in recent years as MOFCOM has assumed the bureaucratic lead on export control issues. For example, the MFA no longer leads export control investigations. This department is involved in interagency deliberations related to both major and dual-use nuclear, chemical, missile, and conventional military goods.

The MFA has several roles. First and foremost, it participates in interagency decisions about possible exports of controlled items to countries of concern. The MFA's main tasks are to assess the impact of potential exports on both China's existing nonproliferation commitments and its broader foreign relations. China's political relationship with the United States is a common consideration on this issue. MFA officials have noted that they have counseled Chinese companies not to engage in exports of sensitive items, even if permitted under Chinese regulations, because the companies risk being sanctioned by the U.S. government. Although MFA officials regularly claim not to possess a "blacklist" of countries of concern, they also state that such a list informally exists and is well known among MFA officials. Countries on the "informal list" likely include Iraq (pre-2003), Iran, Libya, Pakistan, and regions of military conflict, such as in Africa.[9] During interagency deliberations, the MFA's nonproliferation experts can be asked to issue an official opinion about the impact of a potential export on China's foreign relations and regional stability. The MFA also helps to evaluate the end users for specific

---

[9] China's conventional weapons exports to Sudan in recent years raise questions about the scope and effectiveness of this informal blacklist and how it is actually applied.

deals based on its past experience assessing proliferation risks in other countries. The MFA can task embassy officials in foreign countries to investigate certain end users during the license review process. The department of arms control possesses a database, built from the department's past work, of some 300 end users throughout the world.

Beyond its role in the licensing process, the MFA also is active in the effort to educate Chinese companies about the government's official nonproliferation policies and laws, and the companies' corresponding responsibilities. MFA officials regularly participate in export-control training seminars throughout China. MFA officials can also issue special documents, such as "red letter documents" (*hong tou xin,* 红头信), which notify Chinese companies and provincial authorities on an urgent basis about certain items that cannot be exported—including goods not included on Chinese control lists. These documents can be issued based on intelligence received from foreign governments about pending illicit exports. The MFA plays a supporting role in the actual investigations of illicit exports. It serves as a conduit of foreign intelligence about impending exports to MOFCOM officials who initiate such investigations. In the past, MFA officials have actually participated in such investigations, and in very few cases conveyed the results of such investigations back to foreign governments.

General Administration of Customs

China's General Administration of Customs (GAC, 海关总署)[10] is another top-tier actor in China's WMD export control system. Customs comprises about 46,000 customs officers located in 41 customs houses located throughout China. In addition, Customs supervises 300 affiliated customs houses and 245 ports in China. Its headquarters is in Beijing, with the Policy and Laws Department (*Zhengfa Si,* 政法司) handling export control issues. China's Customs agency has

---

[10] The new head of China's Customs Authority is a career officer in China's Ministry of Public Security, which could improve Customs' role in export control enforcement.

jurisdiction over customs surveillance areas and designated surrounding areas; it can conduct inspections and seizures (of people or vehicles) only in these types of areas. (Outside those areas, the China Ministry of Public Security has jurisdiction.)[11]

Similar to the customs agencies in other countries, China's Customs clearance is the final point of contact for any export before leaving the country. Its role is to inspect items crossing China's borders to ensure that proper government permissions and licenses have been given to prevent the transfer abroad of banned items or controlled goods. This authority is laid out in Article 40 of China Customs Law and further specified in various nonproliferation regulations. Foreign Ministry materials describe Customs' role as follows:

> Where an application is examined and approved, the Ministry of Commerce shall issue a license and notify the Customs in writing. The Customs shall proceed, according to relevant laws and regulations, with the formalities and supervise the entire process so as to ensure that the category and quantity of exported items are identical with the declaration.[12]

Customs Officer Wu Genping (deputy division director in Customs' Department of Policy and Regulations), in a presentation in Shanghai in 2003, specified Customs' role in controlling exports of sensitive items. He identified three stages:

1. At the time of export, exporters should voluntarily present the export license to the Customs officer. Exporters failing to do so will be solely responsible for the legal consequences. When neces-

---

[11] For more information, see Jonathan E. Davis, *Export Controls of the People's Republic of China 2005*, Athens, Ga.: Center for International Trade and Security, University of Georgia, February 2005. According to this report, Customs can detain suspects for 24 to 48 hours based on suspicions.

[12] See "Statement by the Chinese Delegation at the Meeting of Experts of the Biological Weapons Convention (BWC) on National Implementation Measures—Export Control Regime, (August 20, 2003, Geneva)," Permanent Mission of the People's Republic of China to the United Nations Office at Geneva and Other International Organizations in Switzerland (http://genevamissiontoun.fmprc.gov.cn/eng/54934.html [English]; http://www.mfa.gov.cn/chn/gjwt/cjjk/default.htm [Chinese]; last accessed April 25, 2005).

sary, the Customs officer can directly request to see the export license. A Customs officer can also demand that those who do not have an export license apply for one at the Ministry of Commerce.

2. The administrative procedures of export licenses for sensitive material and technologies are still being established. Hence, exporters should present the Customs officer with the export license for appropriate processing.

3. The license includes the main document as an attachment. The Customs officer collects one-time export licenses for processing and filing purposes. On multi-item export licenses, the Customs officer will indicate on the back of the attachment the amount being cleared, the date, the Customs officer's name, and will then retain the carbon copy. When the multi-item export license expires or when the maximum quantity for export has been reached, the Customs officer will collect for processing and filing.

Most of Customs' efforts in recent years have been focused on anti-smuggling—a high priority among China's leadership. As a result of this preoccupation, the GAC suffers from several weaknesses that have hindered its ability to monitor and stop illicit exports of controlled sensitive items. Thus, this has become a weak point in China's export control system. The key limitations in Customs capabilities include a lack of knowledge of Chinese export control regulations by Customs officials, a lack of technical knowledge to evaluate proscribed exports, a lack of understanding of the importance of government nonproliferation policies, and endemic corruption. The latter consideration is a pervasive problem that will not be easily resolved; numerous Chinese officials and analysts note that corruption is a major and enduring weakness of China's current export control system—at the Customs level of operations and beyond.

Customs' roles and capabilities have begun to change, and it has become more actively involved in the administration of nonproliferation export controls. Several important steps are noteworthy. First, the government in the past few years has set up a numerical commodity control system (*chukou mulu guanli daihao xitong*, 出口目录管理代码系统), which assigns numbers to categories of high-tech goods—only some of which are controlled exports requiring a license.[13] This technical development is important because it dramatically reduces the type of specific knowledge needed for effective customs controls. Theoretically, any Customs officer, regardless of age or experience, can utilize the commodity control number to determine whether an export license is needed for the item being inspected. The system is still evolving, however. Customs officials have stated that, to date, only 30 percent of controlled sensitive items have been issued such harmonized codes.

Customs has broadened its role in WMD export control administration, such as those related to inspections, training, and investigations. According to one report,[14] some Customs "clearance zones" in recent years have acquired specialized equipment to detect radiological, biological, and chemical items. This equipment includes X-ray machines, electronic platform balances, plate identification systems, electronic gates, and container identification systems. While these developments are important, they have occurred at China's largest ports, such as in Shanghai, and have been driven by a desire to monitor imports, likely as part of the Container Security Initiative. It is not clear that many Customs border-houses throughout the country possess such technology and the ability to fully exploit it. MOFCOM officials and Customs officials have specifically raised the issue of inconsistent inspection capabilities at sites across China.[15]

Customs training has involved educating its personnel about the importance of nonproliferation in their daily duties; admittedly, much more work is needed in this area. Customs lacks sufficient numbers of qualified personnel, equipment, and experience. In 2003–

---

[13] The GAC currently has eight categories of high-tech goods that are assigned commodity classification numbers. Not all of these are controlled items that require an export license. The eight categories are (1) information technology; (2) software; (3) aviation and aerospace technologies; (4) fiber-optic integration technologies; (5) biomedicine and medical equipment; (6) new material (*xin cailiao*, 新材料); (7) new energy resources and energy-preservation products; and (8) technologies (including environmental protection technologies).

[14] Davis, 2005.

[15] Interview with Chinese official, Beijing, China, October 2004.

2004, Customs officials started to participate in export control seminars. MOFCOM held a Customs training seminar in May 2004 in Northeastern China to educate local Customs officials about the relevant laws and regulations related to WMD export control. Customs Officer Wu Genping gave a presentation at the joint U.S.-China Customs seminar in Shanghai in September 2003; this was the first public presentation by a Customs official about WMD export controls. Customs officials have also traveled to the United States to study WMD export control issues as part of their training.

Customs has assumed a more active role in investigations to prevent illicit WMD exports. In 2004, Customs became part of the interagency team that investigates and tracks down pending illicit exports. Customs is also part of the rapid-response interagency team established in 2003 to handle urgent cases. Thus, more attention and resources have been devoted to Customs' role in export control of sensitive WMD goods and technologies. Another critical aspect of evaluating Customs' capabilities is assessing their activities at both the provincial and local levels. Yet, very little is known about those dimensions of Customs' operations.

China Atomic Energy Agency

The China Atomic Energy Agency (CAEA, 中国原子能机构)[16] is the government's main point of contact for licensing exports of nuclear *materials*, nuclear *equipment*, and *non-nuclear goods* used in nuclear power reactors.[17] (By contrast, CAEA is not the lead agency for vetting *dual-use* nuclear exports.)

This role is specified in several government regulations (*tiaoli*, 条例) on nuclear exports published in 1987 and 1997. CAEA's

---

[16] CAEA is officially part of China's COSTIND, but it is listed separately here because of its distinct role in nuclear export licensing decisions. See the CAEA Web site at www.caea.gov.cn (Chinese) or http://www.caea.gov.cn/ecaea/index.asp (English) for more information.

[17] The decisionmaking for each of these three categories of items is slightly different.

Department of International Cooperation (*Guoji Hezuo Si,* 国际合作司) is responsible for running, in conjunction with MOFCOM, the export license application and review process. Chinese companies are required to apply to CAEA for (1) general authority to export controlled nuclear items and (2) a license to export a specific nuclear item controlled under the relevant regulations. In practical terms, CAEA's responsibilities and activities are fairly limited. The government has authorized a very small number of nuclear industry companies to export such nuclear-specific items.[18] Actual exports of such items also are very limited. A single nuclear-industry company is involved in one project in Pakistan to build the Chasma-2 power reactor, based on the only Chinese-designed reactor.

CAEA licensing decisions are often made in consultation with other government agencies. Once CAEA has received a license application, depending on the end use and end user, it consults with its nuclear experts as well as both MOFCOM and the MFA. The latter two organizations often provide advice about end users but rely on CAEA's technical experts for end-use evaluations. If an affirmative decision has been made, the license application is forwarded to MOFCOM's Licensing Bureau, where a formal license is issued. Given CAEA's technical expertise in nuclear issues, its experts can be tapped to provide advice and formal opinions to MOFCOM during deliberations about possible exports of controlled, dual-use nuclear goods. CAEA officials also participate in all levels of discussions about change or modifications to China nuclear export control regulations or additional nuclear nonproliferation commitments, such as membership in the NSG. CAEA personnel have also participated in training courses on export controls with the United States in September 2003 in Shanghai and government-to-government export control consultations with the United States in May 2004 in Beijing.

---

[18] The main nuclear industry exporter is the China Nuclear Import-Export Corporation (CNIEC); it possesses a few subsidiaries that have engaged in authorized nuclear exports.

Chemical Weapons Convention Implementation Office

The Chemical Weapons Convention Implementation Office (CWCIO, 禁止化学办公室), which is currently located within China's State Development and Reform Commission (*Guojia Fazhan Gaige Weiyuanhui,* 国家发展改革委员会 or 国家发改委), is the main point of contact for reviewing possible exports of major chemical goods controlled under the CWC.[19] It employs some 20 to 30 people. The office is at the same bureaucratic level as a department (*siji danwei,* 司机单位) in a government ministry (*bumen,* 部门). The titular head of the CWCIO is a vice premier; this unusual step was taken in order to give the CWCIO the authority it needs to implement CWC compliance at the provincial level. The CWCIO operates provincial offices in Shanghai, Tianjin, Wuhan, and other major cities.

    The office's main responsibility, and the one that consumes most of its time and resources, is to carry out and administer China's compliance with the CWC. This includes facilitating visits of inspectors from the Hague-based Organization for the Prohibition of Chemical Weapons. In terms of export controls, China's CWCIO is responsible for preventing the export of all CWC-controlled items. Curiously, this office is also responsible for vetting possible exports of the ten dual-use chemical items from the AG, which China placed on its control list in June 1998.[20] The CWCIO is also actively involved in the training and educating of China's chemical industry companies; it has held seminars in various provinces in recent years and worked with MOFCOM to increase awareness of China's export controls and obligations. Educating China's chemical industry is a particularly daunting task due to the large size and widely dispersed nature of the chemical industry in China. Much of the chemical industry has never

---

[19] China signed the CWC on January 13, 1993. In December 1996, the Standing Committee of the 8th National People's Congress approved ratification of the CWC and deposited its instrument of ratification with the Secretary General of the United Nations on April 25, 1997 ("China Profiles" database at www.nti.org).

[20] Dozens of other dual-use chemicals were added in 2002.

before been under government control, which has further complicated the government's ability to inform it about changes in government laws and regulations.

Commission on Science, Technology, and Industry for National Defense

The Commission on Science, Technology, and Industry for National Defense (COSTIND, 国防科工委) is the government's main organ in charge of oversight of China's defense industrial enterprises (*jungong qiye,* 军工企业). COSTIND serves as the main administrative and regulatory point of contact for China's defense industries. COSTIND is a civilian agency under the State Council, although from its inception in 1982 until 1998 it was both a civilian and a military organ linked to the Chinese military. As a national-level government organ, it has offices in almost every province of China.

COSTIND is the main point of contact for licensing decisions for conventional military exports—including exports of complete ballistic and cruise missiles covered by China's various missile nonproliferation pledges. (As was mentioned earlier, MOFCOM is in charge of vetting exports of dual-use aerospace and missile goods.) COSTIND's export control responsibilities are outlined in 1997 regulations on military exports and its corresponding control list, both of which were updated in 2002.[21] Chinese companies seeking to export controlled conventional military goods are required to apply to COSTIND for an export license. According to COSTIND, only nine Chinese companies (see Figure 4.9 in Chapter Four) are officially authorized by the government to engage in export of controlled military items.

In contrast to the nuclear and chemical export licensing processes, MOFCOM is not involved *in any phase* of licensing for conventional military exports. Once COSTIND decides to issue a

---

[21] The list incorporates the Wassenar Group control list, but not the group's list of dual-use goods and technologies.

license for a military export, it has a special licensing bureau for military exports that issues the license and sends a notification to the Customs agency. COSTIND's decisions about military exports are located in the military export office (*Junmao Ban,* 军贸办) within COSTIND's Department of International Cooperation (*Guoji Hezuo Si,* 国际合作司).

COSTIND also plays a role in vetting possible exports of nuclear *materials* (uranium, plutonium, and others) in conjunction with the CAEA, after which an application is rejected or forwarded to MOFCOM for further consideration (Chapter Four provides further information on this process).

Given COSTIND's position as the defense industry's main point of contact, it has also been involved in the national effort to educate defense industry companies about government regulations and industry obligations. It has convened seminars and invited MOFCOM and MFA officials to provide presentations on China's nonproliferation commitments. The existence of COSTIND offices at the provincial level may have assisted this process because those offices can serve as local points of contact and assistance for China's numerous defense enterprises.

However, COSTIND's mandate as the chief promoter and defender of defense industry interests places it in direct conflict with its emerging export control responsibilities. COSTIND's leadership has a vested interest in the growth and development of defense industrial enterprises, which may not always be consistent with its role as the sole authority for vetting conventional military and missile exports.

This conflict of interest raises questions about COSTIND's effectives in the export control process and the degree to which the government has incentivized it to pay close attention to WMD export control. According to China's national 2002 military export regulations, COSTIND's only needs to consult with "the relevant departments of the State Council and the CMC" in the case of "important" exports, although none of those terms are defined in the regulations. Thus, the scope of COSTIND's decisionmaking authority on "major" weapons exports is not well defined, providing ample room for interpretation and latitude.

General Armaments Department of the PLA

The General Armaments Department (GAD, 总装备部) of the PLA has a limited role in decisions about conventional military exports, but its role is far narrower than COSTIND's. First, GAD is consulted when a possible conventional military export could raise national security concerns *related to the PLA's operational capabilities*. If such an item is in China's arsenal, for example, then the GAD is tasked by COSTIND with providing an opinion about whether such an export would compromise an existing PLA military capability. Second, for unclear "historical reasons," some Chinese defense firms (perhaps ones with strong past ties to the PLA) actually go to the GAD for licenses for conventional military exports, and not to COSTIND. This is a unique and strange situation for China and is a result of the fact that COSTIND and GAD, prior to 1998, were one organization. As a result of their splitting in two, this unusual situation of divided licensing authority arose; it is not likely to change given the continuing competition for authority between these two organizations.[22]

Ministry of Public Security/Public Security Bureau

The Ministry of Public Security (MPS, 公安部)/Public Security Bureau (PSB, 公安局)[23] plays a limited but growing role in the enforcement of national export control regulations. It participates in the investigation of pending illegal exports of controlled items or investigates cases after the export has occurred. Its role in export control enforcement has grown in recent years. The MPS/PSB has become increasingly involved in preventing illegal exports, usually when tipped off with information provided by Western intelligence agencies. MPS and PSB officials are now part of a Chinese

---

[22] Interviews with Chinese export control officials, Beijing, China, October 2003.

[23] The MPS is the national level public security organization and the PSB is the provincial branch of the public security apparatus.

government rapid-reaction task force used to stop illicit exports before they leave China. The MPS in Beijing established in early 2003 a special team, within its economic crimes bureau, to handle weapons-related export control cases. Also, if an initial investigation by MOFCOM determines that there was criminal intent in a case (usually involving lying or document falsification or forgery),[24] then the MPS is tasked with conducting a formal criminal investigation of the incident. Once the investigation is complete, MPS theoretically forwards criminal cases to the Procuracy[25] for formal prosecution. Chinese officials stated in spring 2004 that the MPS had already forwarded two such criminal cases related to illicit WMD exports to the Procuracy. However, there is no public information that any such punishments have been issued.

Secondary Actors

Within the Chinese bureaucracy, there is also a host of secondary actors that contribute to the various processes of export control administration, education, implementation, and enforcement. These organs include both government and nominally nongovernmental organizations in the Chinese system. These organs are considered secondary actors in this report because none of them plays a direct role in export control administration; their role is occasional and supportive to official export control decisionmaking processes. In other words, they are sometimes involved in some aspects of licensing decisions and export control enforcement but are not involved at all levels and at all times.

Industry associations (*gongye xiehui,* 工业协会) constitute one group of actors that has contributed to export control admini-

---

[24] Chinese officials have stated that they generally use the same standards that the United States uses for determining when a case involves criminal intent and is passed along to law enforcement authorities.

[25] *Procuracy* is China's term for a prosecutor; the Procuracy exists at every level of government.

stration in China. Associations, which are tied to specific industries, were formed to provide assistance for various industrial activities.[26] The main example of such an organization, which is currently within China's chemical industry, is the China Controlled Chemicals Association (CCCA, 中国监控化学品协会).[27] This broad group, whose members initially numbered 90, was formally established in October 1995 to assist the chemical industry's participation in inspections required for China's compliance with the CWC. It has since grown to more than 150 members. CCCA has helped to inform China's large and dispersed chemical enterprises about the requirements of compliance with the CWC. In the late 1990s, it broadened its role in informing and educating Chinese companies about their export control obligations related to controlled chemicals and related production equipment. In addition, equivalent industry associations are tied to both the nuclear and aerospace industry, but it is not clear whether they assist with export control administration.

The role of such associations may grow in the future. A December 2003 white paper on nonproliferation[28] noted that the government would on an "as needed" basis draw on the technical expertise of an "independent panel of technical experts" to evaluate the proliferation risks of potential exports. Some of these experts may be based in industry associations. The precise role of these technical specialists in vetting possible WMD-related exports is not entirely clear.

Chinese research institutes (*yanjiu jigou*, 研究机构) working on nonproliferation issues have also played a role in export control administration. Chinese nonproliferation specialists from the Chinese Academy of Social Sciences (CASS) and the China Institute of Contemporary International Relations (CICIR) have participated in internal meetings and industry-wide seminars on nonproliferation

---

[26] A Web site on these industry organizations can be found at www.ica.org.cn (Chinese).

[27] For details on this organization, see the China Controlled Chemicals Association Web site (http://www.ica.gov.cn/xh/wgxh/syandhx010/syandhx04.htm; last accessed April 2004).

[28] *China's Non-Proliferation Policy and Measures,* Beijing, China: State Council Information Office, December 2003 (http://www.china.org.cn/e-white/20031202/index.htm; last accessed April 2004).

export controls. In these venues, these specialists have discussed the dangers of WMD proliferation and the importance of effective export control for China's economic development as well as for its foreign policy interests. These specialists outline the policy rationale for enterprises to adhere strictly to Chinese export control regulations—a necessary task in a country where rule of law and strict adherence to regulations are relatively new modes of business operations. These nonproliferation specialists have also conducted independent studies about the U.S. export control systems and ways that China can improve its internal controls. Recently, China's newly formed China Arms Control and Disarmament Association (CACDA) formed a task force to study Western export control practices in order to offer suggestions for the development of China's export control system. While it is difficult to judge the precise influence of China's cadre of nonproliferation specialists, they serve as a force for change and increased attention to nonproliferation and export controls within the Chinese system, at both the government and industry level. This collection of expertise outside formal government departments is a new phenomenon and did not exist ten years ago.

University-based research programs on arms control and nonproliferation issues also broadly contribute to China's national ability to effectively administer export controls on sensitive items. Individuals in these programs are conducting research on export controls and are training students on the policy and technical complexities of such issues. Professor Li Bin at Qinghua University's Institute for International Relations started a program on arms control studies in 2002. Under its auspices, Professor Li teaches M.A.-level and Ph.D.-level courses on arms control and nonproliferation-related issues. Some of his M.A. candidates, for their thesis requirement, have researched both foreign and Chinese export control systems and practice.[29] Upon graduation, Chinese university students can go into government and industry to further China's national understanding of export control administration. Some Chinese professors with such ex-

---

[29] Links to examples of this work can be found on the Arms Control Archive Web site at http://learn.tsinghua.edu.cn/homepage/2000990313/archive.htm.

pertise often participate in internal meetings, including within the defense industry establishment, on export control topics, and they can consult with government agencies as well. These specialists often serve as an internal advocate of effective nonproliferation controls with the Chinese bureaucracy.

In addition to the program at Qinghua University, Fudan University in Shanghai also has an active research program on arms control and nonproliferation; it was the first such program in China. It is housed within the Center for American Studies. Fudan professors Shen Dingli and Zhu Mingquan teach both M.A.- and Ph.D.-level classes on national security, nonproliferation, and arms control. Some of their students are currently employed at MOFCOM and the Foreign Ministry. Last year, MOFCOM approached Fudan's program about conducting academic research on export control issues; MOFCOM also suggested partnering with Fudan to establish a southern export control research center. MOFCOM officials also expressed an interest in setting up a northern export control research center in Beijing, perhaps at Qinghua University. It is not clear whether either venture will materialize.

CHAPTER FOUR

Chinese Export Control Decisionmaking: Registration and Licensing Processes

This chapter outlines the multiple steps involved in China's license application and review process for exports of conventional military goods and WMD-related goods and technologies. It begins with a general overview of China's export control system, including a discussion of the laws, regulations, and measures that guide export control decisionmaking. The chapter then addresses in detail the following five export control processes:

1. Certification of an entity as an authorized exporter of controlled sensitive goods and technologies
2. Nuclear export licensing (including nuclear dual-use items)
3. Chemical export licensing (including chemical dual-use items)
4. Conventional military equipment export licensing
5. Missile goods and technology export licensing (only dual-use).

General Overview of China's Export Control System

This section of the chapter outlines the "big picture" aspects of China's export licensing system regarding sensitive WMD goods and technologies. It sketches the broad processes in the system and the broad legal basis for export control in China. Subsequent sections cover these processes in more detail.

Key Policy Attributes of China's Export Control System

China has gradually created over the years a legally based system for controlling exports of sensitive goods and technologies. Part of this process has involved issuing laws and regulations that have institutionalized China's multilateral and bilateral nonproliferation commitments. Another important step in the process of system-building has been the incorporation of international standards for nonproliferation export control, which in the past were not universally present in China's rules, regulations, and practices. These standards include:

- a registration and licensing system
- control lists of equipment, materials, and technologies
- end-user and end-use certifications
- catch-all principles
- customs supervision
- punishments and penalties.

It has taken literally decades to get to the point at which China not only has in place a complete set of export control regulations, but those regulations all reflect key international export control standards and practices. The next major challenge for China is ensuring that these rules, regulations, practices, and decisionmaking standards are universally utilized and enforced throughout the country. Along these lines, major efforts also need to ensure that the government punishes violators when infractions are uncovered.

Top-Level Legal Basis for Export Controls in China

The legal foundation for export controls on sensitive goods in China is based on several laws. The one of greatest significance is the 1994 Foreign Trade Law (*Duiwai Maoyi Fa,* 对外贸易法). This law, the highest legal instrument in the Chinese system, is the top-level document under which all subsequent *regulations* (*tiaoli,* 条例) and *measures* (*banfa,* 办法) on export control are issued. (However, there has been some discussion on issuing a separate law on WMD export controls.) The 1994 law was one of the first formal and public legal instruments in China to specifically address export control issues;

prior to this law, most controls were internal decrees that were not public and not universally known. The creation of this law in 1994 was the first step in the process of shifting from administrative to legally based export controls. The Foreign Trade Law provides the state with the explicit power to regulate imports and exports and specifies how this will be done. It made these processes transparent and explicit for the first time. Under Articles 16 and 17 of the Foreign Trade Law, the government can restrict or prohibit the import and export of goods for reasons of "safeguarding national security and public interests" and "under the international treaties or agreements signed or acceded to by the People's Republic of China"; Article 18 requires the creation of control lists; and Article 19 provides for licensing authority of items with "special requirements." These stipulations and control lists were then detailed in subsequent regulations that appeared in following years. This law was revised in 2004, and these changes have important implications for the functioning of China's export control system (this issue is addressed later in this chapter).

The Customs Law (*Zhonghua Renmin Gongheguo Haiguan Fa,* 中华人民共和国海关法) is another law relevant to export control in China. This law establishes the legal basis of China's system of customs inspection and verification for import and export trade controls. Additional laws provide the government with further legal basis for export controls and specifically for export control enforcement. They include the Administrative Punishments Law and the 2001 Amendments to the Criminal Law. The latter designates as criminal offenses such acts as illegally trafficking and transporting radioactive substances.

In addition to laws, there are several sets of *regulations, circulars,* and *measures* that further formalize and legalize China's export control system. In December 2003, MOFCOM and Customs jointly issued a circular specifying the procedures for Customs examination of export certificates in Customs' clearance of sensitive items and technologies. The duties and obligations of exporters in meeting Customs' inspections requirements are clearly outlined in this document. In January 2004, MOFCOM issued measures that specify for companies the precise procedures involved in applying for and gaining authority to export sensitive, controlled goods as well as the procedures for applying for a specific export license. They are known as *Provisional Measures on the Administration of the Export License on Sensitive Items and Technologies* and are on MOFCOM's website (www.mofcom.gov.cn [Chinese] and english.mofcom.gov.cn [English]). In 2004, MOFCOM and Customs also jointly issued a catalogue of sensitive goods that require an export license. The issuance of these new procedures and legal instruments is part of the government's effort to establish a firm legal basis for effective export control administration on sensitive goods and technologies.

Broad Outline of China's System of Controls on Sensitive Goods and Technologies

In general terms, there are several steps in the system of government controls on sensitive WMD and military items. A description of these broad steps provides a top-level understanding of how the system works. A detailed drill-down of specific licensing processes (nuclear, chemical, conventional military) is provided in the following paragraphs and in Figure 4.1.

Step 1A: A Chinese company, a joint-venture enterprise, or a wholly owned foreign entity (hereafter referred to as a "Chinese entity") must hold a business license to conduct commercial operations in China.

Step 1B: A Chinese entity must register with MOFCOM and obtain certification for general import/export activities. According to MOFCOM estimates, some 350,000 to 450,000 Chinese companies currently possess such authority.[1]

Step 2: A Chinese entity must apply to MOFCOM's Department of Science and Technology for a general authorization/

---

[1] Under China's revised 2004 Foreign Trade Law, steps 1A and 1B were combined. Thus, when a company receives a business license it will automatically also receive an export/import authorization.

Figure 4.1
Overview of China's Export Licensing System, 2005

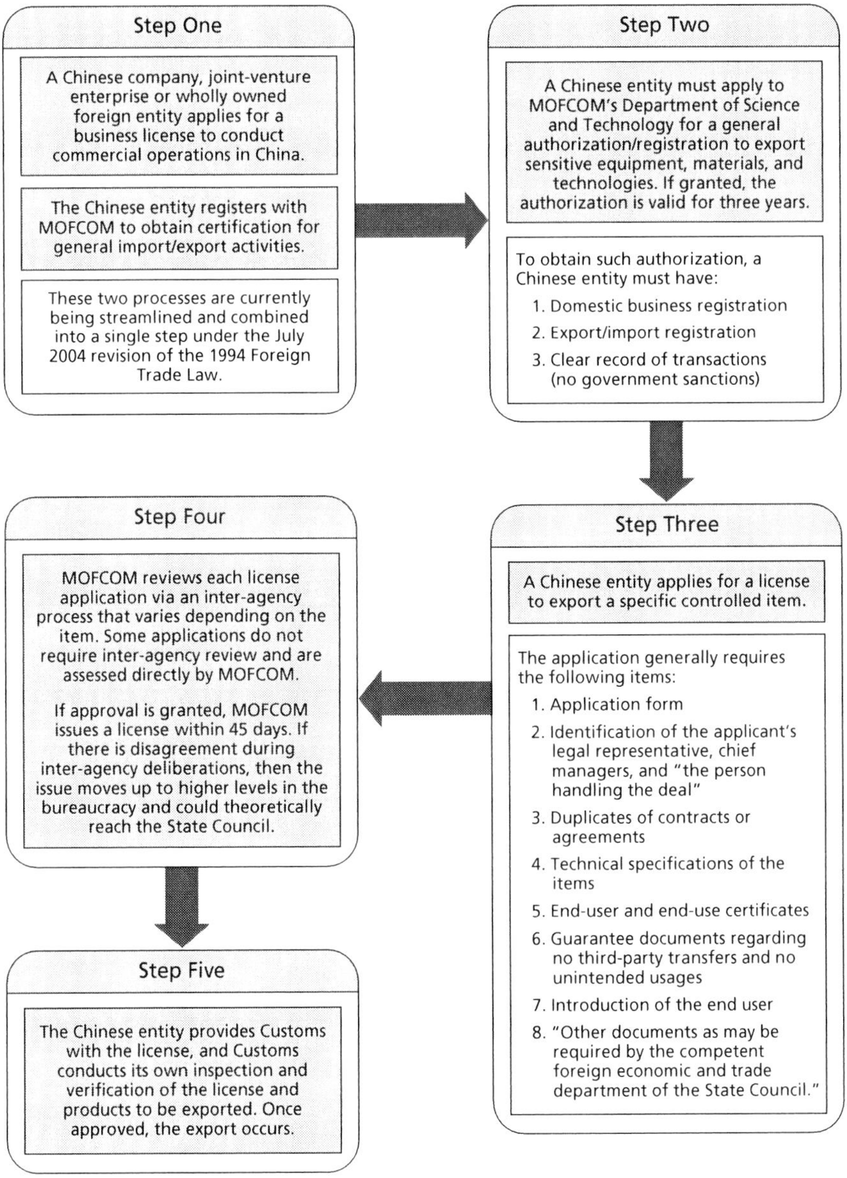

Step One

A Chinese company, joint-venture enterprise or wholly owned foreign entity applies for a business license to conduct commercial operations in China.

The Chinese entity registers with MOFCOM to obtain certification for general import/export activities.

These two processes are currently being streamlined and combined into a single step under the July 2004 revision of the 1994 Foreign Trade Law.

Step Two

A Chinese entity must apply to MOFCOM's Department of Science and Technology for a general authorization/registration to export sensitive equipment, materials, and technologies. If granted, the authorization is valid for three years.

To obtain such authorization, a Chinese entity must have:

1. Domestic business registration
2. Export/import registration
3. Clear record of transactions (no government sanctions)

Step Four

MOFCOM reviews each license application via an inter-agency process that varies depending on the item. Some applications do not require inter-agency review and are assessed directly by MOFCOM.

If approval is granted, MOFCOM issues a license within 45 days. If there is disagreement during inter-agency deliberations, then the issue moves up to higher levels in the bureaucracy and could theoretically reach the State Council.

Step Three

A Chinese entity applies for a license to export a specific controlled item.

The application generally requires the following items:

1. Application form
2. Identification of the applicant's legal representative, chief managers, and "the person handling the deal"
3. Duplicates of contracts or agreements
4. Technical specifications of the items
5. End-user and end-use certificates
6. Guarantee documents regarding no third-party transfers and no unintended usages
7. Introduction of the end user
8. "Other documents as may be required by the competent foreign economic and trade department of the State Council."

Step Five

The Chinese entity provides Customs with the license, and Customs conducts its own inspection and verification of the license and products to be exported. Once approved, the export occurs.

registration to export controlled equipment, materials, and technologies.[2] If granted, this authorization is good for three years. To obtain this authorization, a Chinese entity must have the following:

1. Domestic business registration
2. Export/import registration
3. Clean record of transactions (no government penalties).

Step 3: A Chinese entity applies for a license to export a specific controlled item (i.e., nuclear, chemical, missile, or military). The detailed aspects of each licensing process are outlined later in this chapter. In general terms, the following items are needed to obtain a license for sensitive items (as stated in Chinese regulations):

1. Application form (downloadable from MOFCOM's website)
2. Identification of the applicant's legal representative, chief managers, and "the person(s) handling the deal"
3. Duplicates of the contract or agreement
4. Technical specifications of the items (i.e., nuclear, chemical, missile, or conventional military)
5. End-user and end-use certificates
6. Documents of guarantee assuring no third-party transfers and no unintended usages
7. Introduction of the end user
8. "Other documents as may be required by the competent foreign economic and trade department of the State Council."

Step 4: MOFCOM reviews each license application in an interagency process, which varies depending on the nature of the item. Some license applications do not require interagency review and can be assessed directly by MOFCOM. If approval is granted,

---

[2] This registration procedure specifically applies to exporters of dual-use CW, nuclear and missile items. Exporters of major CW, nuclear, or conventional military items have already been designated by the State Council. These are noted on the charts.

MOFCOM issues a license within 45 days. This step is addressed in more detail later in this chapter.

MOFCOM officials say they group license applications into three categories: approvals, rejections, and gray-area applications. When applications fall into the last category, that of uncertainty, they are sent to other agencies, such as the Foreign Ministry, or to a team of technical experts as part of China's interagency license review system. At this point, MOFCOM may also task foreign embassies to conduct investigations of potential end users. MOFCOM may also request additional data from the Chinese company about the end use or end user.

During this interagency review process, the Chinese government has specified the policy standards that are used to evaluate each application. In past years, it was unclear what standards were used and which organizations played a role in evaluating them. Although these standards have been specified, it is not known how rigorously the government adheres to them. These standards are as follows:

- China's international nonproliferation obligations
- China's national security and social and public interests
- Chinese foreign policy interests
- The regional security situation of the recipient
- The WMD activities of the recipient and whether the transfer would contribute to proliferation in the host nation or could be re-transferred to a potential proliferator
- The recipient is subject to United Nations (UN) sanctions
- The recipient's links to international terrorism (a new standard added in December 2003)
- The situation of the end-user in the host nation.[3]

If there is disagreement during interagency deliberations, then the issue gets moved up to higher levels in the bureaucracy. It begins at the division level (*chuji*, 处级), can move to the department level

---

[3] These standards are outlined in a subsequent section of the study.

(*siji*, 司级), then to the ministry level (*bumen*, 部门), and then, theoretically, to the level of the State Council. Chinese officials have stated that disagreements seldom go above the level of director generals of various departments (*si zhang*, 司长), although this has been known to occur, according to Chinese officials.

Once the export is approved, MOFCOM issues the license and informs Customs in writing about the license.

Step 5: The Chinese entity provides Customs with the license, and Customs conducts its own inspection and verification of the license and the products to be exported. Once approved, the export occurs. If no license is required, it is the responsibility of the enterprise to provide Customs with proof that this is the case. Customs can hold an item until the enterprise gets a written authorization to this effect from MOFCOM.[4]

Nuclear Export Control Licensing Process

This section first outlines the licensing process for nuclear and dual-use nuclear exports and then describes the process in more detail. Figure 4.2 highlights the various organizations involved in the nuclear vetting process, and Figures 4.3, 4.4, and 4.5 depict the license application and approval processes.

The legal foundation for controls on nuclear and nuclear dual-use equipment, materials, and technologies is based on several regulations (listed on pages 54–55) that were promulgated as early as 1987. Significant progress on improving nuclear export controls occurred in 1997 in the run-up to the fall presidential summit between Bill Clinton and Jiang Zemin. The United States required that China adopt such export control regulations in order for the United States to activate the dormant bilateral agreement on peaceful uses of nuclear technology (PUNT).

---

[4] Various applications and certificates related to these processes are in the appendices to this report. The source for these items is MOFCOM's export control Web site.

Figure 4.2
Government Organizations Overseeing Export Control Decisionmaking for Nuclear-Specific Goods, 2005

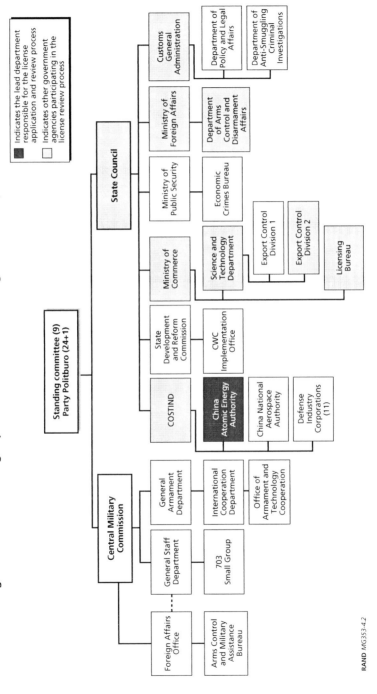

■ Indicates the lead department responsible for the license application and review process

□ Indicates other government agencies participating in the license review process

Figure 4.3
Export Control Licensing Process for Nuclear-Specific Goods

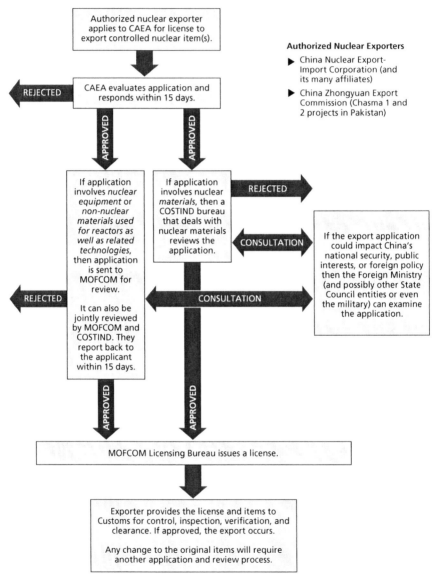

Authorized Nuclear Exporters

▶ China Nuclear Export-
   Import Corporation (and
   its many affiliates)

▶ China Zhongyuan Export
   Commission (Chasma 1 and
   2 projects in Pakistan)

RAND *MG353-4.3*

NOTE: This figure is based on *Chinese Regulations on Nuclear Export Control* (2001 Revision).

Figure 4.4
Licensing Process for Nuclear Materials

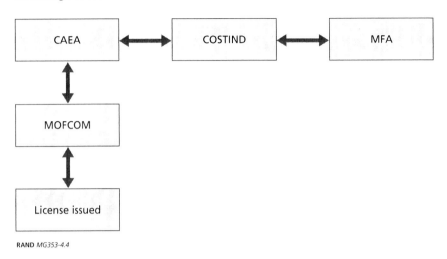

RAND *MG353-4.4*

Figure 4.5
Licensing Process for Nuclear Equipment and Non-Nuclear Materials Used for Reactors

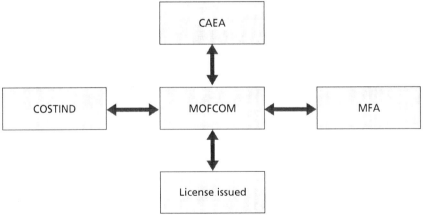

RAND *MG353-4.5*

Regulations on the Control of Nuclear Material (*He Cailiao Guanli Tiaoli,* 核材料管理条例). These were China's first regulations governing the export of nuclear materials (e.g., uranium, plutonium, heavy water) and were issued in 1987, four years after China joined the IAEA, in an effort to better manage and regulate the use of nuclear materials. They did not cover nuclear equipment or related technologies.

Circular on Strict Implementation of China's Nuclear Export Policy. This document, issued in May 1997, was China's first effort to move beyond internal control and to broaden public controls beyond nuclear materials. The circular stated: "The nuclear materials, nuclear equipment, and related technology, as well as non-nuclear materials for reactors and nuclear-related dual-use equipment, materials, and relevant technologies on China's export list must not be supplied to or used in nuclear facilities not under IAEA safeguards. No agency or company is allowed to conduct cooperation or exchange of personnel and technological data with nuclear facilities not under IAEA safeguards."

Regulations on Nuclear Export Control (2001 Revision) (*He Chukou Guanli Tiaoli,* 核出口管理条例). These regulations, issued in September 1997, were more authoritative and detailed than the May 1997 circular. They outlined the specific processes and requirements for licensing major nuclear exports. The regulations also included, for the first time, a control list that virtually matched the one used by the NSG (the official name of the NSG control list is INFCIRC/254 Part I). The regulations were revised in 2001 to improve the controls. The government recently reissued the regulations in late 2003 with corresponding eight-digit commodity classification numbers to assist the Customs clearance process.

Regulations on Export Control of Dual-Use Nuclear Products and Related Technologies (*He Liangyongpin Ji Xiangguan Jishu Chukou Guanli Tiaoli,* 核两用品及相关技术出口管制条例). These regulations, promulgated in June 1998, closed a major loophole in China's nuclear export control system. Until 1998, exports of dual-use nuclear products were not well monitored. The regulations also include a detailed control list identical to the dual-use list used by the NSG (INFCIRC/254 Part II). This control list was recently reissued with corresponding commodity control numbers. These regulations include an important new aspect: a "catch-all" clause that allows the government to deny any export regardless of whether it is on a control list. Indeed, the regulations do not specify a precise trigger for the catch-all clause, which provides the government with wide authority to cancel pending exports. This latter element goes beyond NSG requirements.

Major Nuclear Export Licensing Process

The licensing process for major nuclear exports has several steps; the items covered in this process include nuclear materials, nuclear equipment, and non-nuclear equipment used in reactor production. The specific items are listed in the control list for the 1997 (revised 2001) Nuclear Export Control Regulations and correspond to the NSG "trigger" (control) list. This licensing process is different from the one for dual-use nuclear exports. (See Figures 4.3 through 4.5.)

Step 1: An authorized nuclear exporter applies to the CAEA for a license to export a controlled nuclear item. CAEA is the lead agency regarding exports of nuclear materials, nuclear equipment, and non-nuclear materials used for reactors. As stated in the regulation, CAEA "shall offer an examination report and notify the applicant within 15 working days after the receipt of the nuclear export application form."[5]

Step 2: If the application involves nuclear *materials*, then a special nuclear materials bureau within COSTIND reviews the license application.

If the application involves *nuclear equipment or non-nuclear materials used for reactors as well as related technologies*, then the application is sent to MOFCOM; MOFCOM can send it to COSTIND for technical review and appraisal. COSTIND and MOFCOM must report within 15 days to the applicant.

---

[5] According to Chinese officials, only two companies are authorized to export major nuclear products—China Nuclear Export-Import Corporation (CNEIC) and China Zhongyuan Export Corporation (CZEC) (see Figure 4.3).

In special circumstances, if CAEA, COSTIND, and MOFCOM need to extend the time limit for license review, another 15 working days may be used. However, the applicant needs to be notified of the extension.

Step 3: If the export application could impact China's national security, public interests, or foreign policy, then CAEA, MOFCOM, and COSTIND will consult with the Foreign Ministry (and possibly other State Council entities or even the PLA) to seek their opinion.

Step 4: If the application is approved, MOFCOM's licensing bureau issues a license and sends a notification to Customs. Any change to the original application will require another full review.

Step 5: The exporter provides the license to Customs for inspection and verification, and the export occurs. Any change to the original application will require another full review.

Dual-Use Nuclear Export Licensing Process

The license review process governing dual-use nuclear exports is a bit different from the process described above for major nuclear exports. MOFCOM is the lead agency in this process, and COSTIND via CAEA provides technical support. Also, the regulations governing such exports include a "catch-all" clause that provides the government with broader authority to cancel exports based on proliferation concerns—regardless of whether an item is on a control list. (See Figures 4.6 and 4.7.)

Step 1: A certified exporter applies to MOFCOM for a license to export a dual-use nuclear item. The application must include all the documents specified above in Step 3 under "Broad Outline of China's System of Controls on Sensitive Goods and Technologies."[6]

---

[6] There is one exception to this requirement in the regulations. According to Article 9, "Where the nuclear dual-use items and related technologies to be exported are for exhibition or for the Chinese party's own use abroad and will be re-imported thereafter within a specified time limit, the related documents provided for in Article 8 of these Regulations may be exempted from being submitted after examination and approval by the MOFCOM when making the application."

Figure 4.6
Government Organizations Overseeing Export Control Decisionmaking for Dual-Use Nuclear Goods, 2005

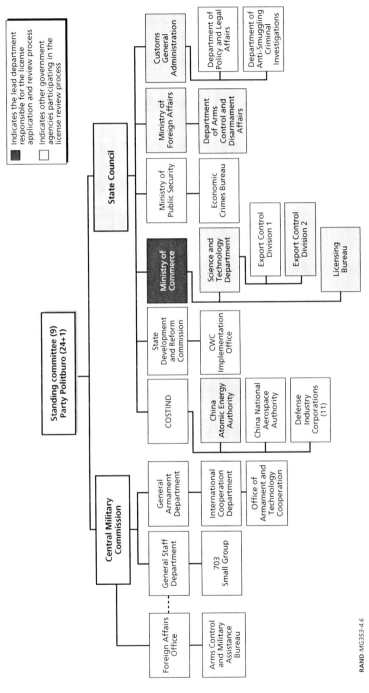

Figure 4.7
Export Control Licensing Process for Dual-Use Nuclear Goods

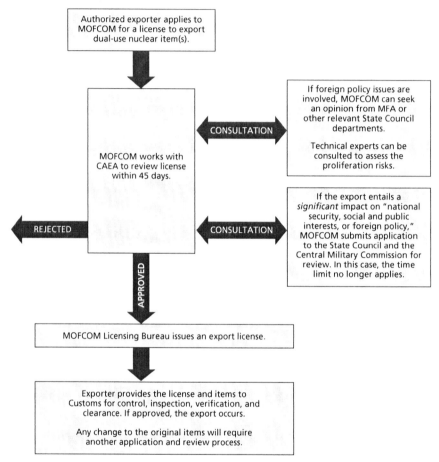

RAND *MG353-4.7*

NOTE: Based on the 1998 Chinese Regulations on Nuclear Dual-Use Items and Related Technologies Export Control.

Step 2: MOFCOM works with CAEA to review the license within 45 days. Technical experts within the Chinese system can be consulted. If foreign policy concerns are involved, MOFCOM can seek an opinion from MFA or other relevant State Council departments.

Step 3: As stated in the regulation on dual-use nuclear exports, if the export has an important impact on "national security, social and public interests, or foreign policy," MOFCOM shall submit it to the State Council for review; in this case, the time limit no longer applies.

Step 4: If the application is approved, then MOFCOM's Licensing Bureau issues a license and sends a notification to Customs. Any change to the original application will require another full review.

The license can also be suspended or revoked. As stated in the regulation, "Where the receiving party contravenes the guarantees made according to the provisions of Article 6 of these Regulations or where a danger of nuclear proliferation appears, MOFCOM shall, after consulting with the Ministry of Foreign Affairs and CAEA, suspend or revoke the export license already granted and notify the Customs in writing for execution."

Step 5: The exporter provides the license to Customs for inspection and verification, and the export occurs. Any change to the original application will require another full review.

Conventional Military Export Control Licensing Process

Chinese export of military products has long been an issue of controversy for China's foreign affairs. China's sales of military equipment to Iran and Iraq in the 1980s first raised China's profile as a major commercial exporter of military products. China's sales of Silkworm missiles to Iran in the late 1980s and ballistic missiles to Pakistan in the early 1990s caused much concern in the United States and in the international community. To coordinate its commercial arms sales with China's changing foreign policy interests, China developed in the early 1990s a nascent system of internal controls on arms sales.

China established in 1992 a high-level organ (at the level of the Central Military Commission [CMC] and State Council) known as the *Military Exports Leading Small Group* (*Junpin Chukou Lingdao Xiaozu,* 军品出口领导小组); it addressed all controversial sales of sensitive weapons exports.[7] Within the General Staff Department of the PLA, an arms trade office acted as the secretariat for this high-level leading group. The MFA also became involved in assessing the foreign policy implications of such export decisions. It is not clear whether the Leading Small Group for military exports still exists or whether it was folded into another interagency coordination body.

China's bureaucratic mechanisms for controlling such exports became more explicit and formal in October 1997 when China issued its first public regulations of military product exports, called the *Regulations on Export Control of Military Products* (*Junpin Chukou Guanli Tiaoli,* 军品出口管理条例). This document outlined the licensing and approval process for military exports. These regulations suffered from many weaknesses, some of which were exploited by Chinese arms exporters.[8] The most notable weakness was the lack of a control list. Some of these problems were addressed when the regulations were amended and improved in December 2002. Certain aspects of the internal review and approval process were clarified to reduce opportunities for Chinese entities to exploit ambiguities, and the revised regulations included a control list as well.[9] The arms export licensing process outlined below reflects the 2002 revisions. (See Figures 4.8 and 4.9.)

Step 1: An authorized arms-trading enterprise[10] submits "*proposals* for arms exports in the form of an application for examination" to

---

[7] In its initial incarnation, this Leading Small Group was jointly headed by General Liu Huaqing and the vice premier in charge of China's defense industry, Zou Jiahua.

[8] Evan S. Medeiros and Bates Gill, *Chinese Arms Exports: Policy, Process and Players*, Carlisle, Pa.: Strategic Studies Institute, U.S. Army War College, August 2000.

[9] The Chinese control list incorporated the Wassenar Group List.

[10] "An arms trading company" as defined in the regulations is "a legal person or enterprise that has obtained according to law the business operations right for arms export and is engaged in arms export business activities within the approved scope of business."

COSTIND or its successor entity. The 2002 revised version of the 1997 regulations outlines many of the specific obligations of "arms trading firms" in the license application process—offering an indication of previous ways that Chinese firms have tried to circumvent government controls.[11]

Step 2: The proposals are reviewed and approved or rejected by COSTIND, possibly in joint consultation with other departments in the State Council and the CMC.

If foreign policy issues are involved, then the MFA will be asked for an opinion. It is up to COSTIND to determine whether to consult the MFA; this judgment is likely contingent on the political climate in China for nonproliferation adherence. In addition, when the item to be exported could affect China's own military capability, the General Armaments Department is consulted to assess the impact on China's national security interests.

Step 3: If a proposal is approved, then the Chinese company can conclude a contract. It must then file another application for review with COSTIND. This review is supposed to take 20 days from receipt of the application. A contract for arms export shall become effective only after it is approved by COSTIND. When the Chinese company files the application with the contract, valid certification documents from the recipient country are necessary (i.e., end-user and end-use certificate).

---

[11] These controls are stated as follows in *Regulations on Export Control of Military Products:*

Article 10: An arms trading company shall honor contracts, guarantee the quality of goods, and improve post-sale services.

Article 11: In accordance with the provisions of the competent arms export department of the State, an arms trading company shall truthfully present the documents and data pertinent to its arms export business activities. The competent arms export department of the State shall keep business secrets of the arms trading company and protect its lawful rights and interests.

Article 12: An arms trading company may entrust an approved transportation enterprise for arms export with the transportation of arms for export and related business matters. Specific measures shall be formulated by the competent arms export department of the State.

Figure 4.8
Government Organizations Overseeing Export Control Decisionmaking for Conventional Military Goods, 2005

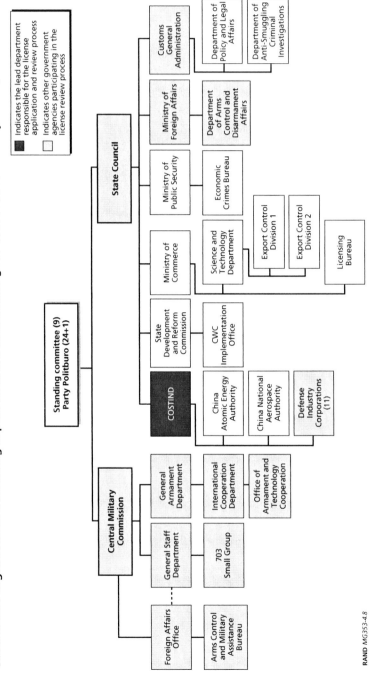

RAND MG353-4.8

Figure 4.9
Export Control Licensing Process for Conventional Military Goods

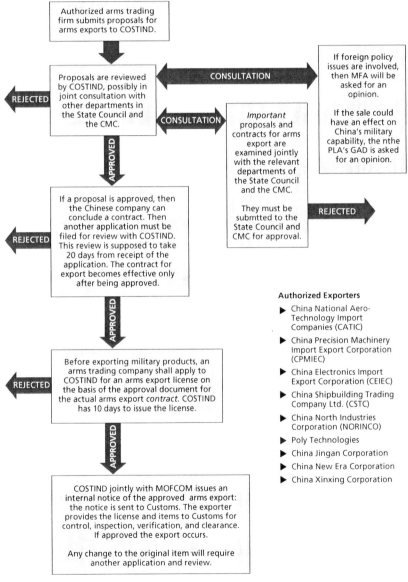

NOTE: Based on *Chinese Regulations on Military Products Exports* (revised 2002).

Step 4: *Important proposals* and contracts for arms export shall be examined jointly by COSTIND with the relevant departments of the State Council and the Central Military Commission, and then must be submitted to the State Council and the Central Military Commission for approval. [It is not clear what distinguishes *proposals* from *important proposals*; perhaps the distinction is similar to that between *military export* and *major military export* in the 1997 version of the regulations.]

Step 5: Before exporting military products, an arms trading company shall apply to COSTIND for an arms export license on the basis of the approval document for the arms export contract. COSTIND has ten days to issue the license. COSTIND has its own licensing bureau; companies do not get an export license from MOFCOM.

Step 6: Customs shall examine the license and give clearance for the export to proceed. COSTIND and concerned departments then will issue an internal notice of the approved arms export. The purpose of this notice is to communicate to other government departments and to provincial and local governments that this arms export can move forward.[12]

Dual-Use Missile Export Licensing Process

Controls on dual-use, missile-related goods and technologies constitute one of the newest areas of export licensing for China. The United States pushed and prodded China for more than a decade to develop regulations governing the export of dual-use missile products. China was reluctant to take this step for years due to the linkages, in China's eyes, between U.S. arms sales to Taiwan and China's non-proliferation pledges. China finally issued a formal missile control regulation in August 2002. Its title is *Regulations on the Export Control of Missiles and Missile-related Items and Technologies*

---

[12] This last step is likely a safeguard against the unknowing complicity by other government agencies and local officials in illegal arms exports.

(中华人民共和国导弹及相关物项和技术出口管制条例.) It de-tails a license application process similar to those outlined above. The regulation importantly includes catch-all provisions. Those regulations state that the exports can be stopped if there is risk of proliferation; they also specify that items not listed in the control list can be subject to control. These regulations, in particular, are a vast improvement from the first missile nonproliferation pledges that China adopted in the early 1990s.[13] The application and licensing review process proceeds in the following manner (see Figures 4.10 and 4.11).

Step 1: A registered Chinese exporter must submit an application for export of a controlled item to MOFCOM. The application must include the standard set of certifications and documents outlined above in Step Three under "Broad Outline of China's System of Controls on Sensitive Goods and Technologies."

Step 2: MOFCOM will review the application within 45 days. MOFCOM can also review it in conjunction with other State Council and CMC organizations. As indicated above, MOFCOM can consult with the MFA and the military depending on the nature of the export and the recipient.

Step 3: If the export "entails significant impact on" China's national security interests or its "social and public interests," then the application is submitted directly to the State Council and CMC for review. It is possibly submitted to a joint CMC–State Council organ involved in vetting arms sales.[14] The 45-day limit does not apply in this instance.

Step 4: If the application is examined and approved by MOFCOM or through an interagency process, MOFCOM issues a license. MOFCOM must also notify Customs after issuing the license.

---

[13] China pledged during bilateral consultations with the United States in November 1991 that it "intends to abide by the guidelines and parameters of the MTCR." That commitment was subsequently codified in a letter to President Bush in spring 1992.

[14] In the past, such an organization existed in the form of a military products Leading Small Group, but it is not clear that this entity still exists or what, if anything, replaced it.

Figure 4.10
Government Organizations Overseeing Export Control Decisionmaking for Dual-Use Missile-Related Goods and Technologies, 2005

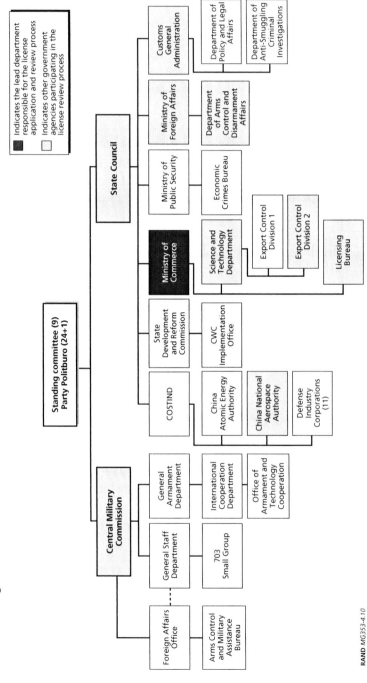

Figure 4.11
Export Control Licensing Process for Dual-Use Missile-Related Goods and Technologies

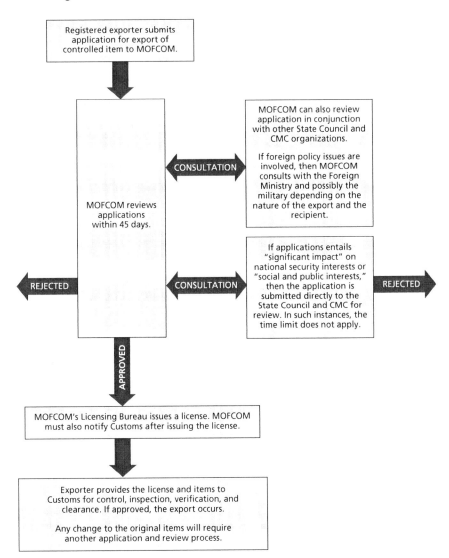

RAND *MG353-4.11*

NOTE: This figure is based on the 2002 Chinese *Regulations on the Export Control of Missiles and Missile-Related Items and Technologies.*

Step 5: The exporter presents the license to Customs. After Customs inspection and verification, the export can proceed. Any change to the original application will require another full review.

Chemical Weapons–Related Export Control Licensing Process

China's controls on CW-related equipment, materials, and technologies were some of the first nonproliferation-related export control regulations ever adopted by the Chinese government. These regulations were part of China's effort to prepare for its 1996 ratification of the CWC. The system of government controls on CW-related exports has evolved significantly since then. The government bureaucracy has changed, and China has increased the scope of its controls on CW-related items. This has resulted in a two-tiered system of controls on CW-related items (see Figures 4.12 through 4.15).

The first tier comprises China's CWCIO, which serves as the main point of contact for exports of CWC-controlled chemicals plus the ten dual-use chemicals added in 1998. The second tier is MOFCOM; it serves as the main point of contact for exports of dual-use CW-related equipment and technology and the chemicals and related equipment that China added in 2002. Thus, the licensing authority for CW goods and technologies is essentially split. There is supposed to be extensive contact between these two organizations during the decisionmaking processes.

Tier One: CWCIO Controls[15]

The legal basis for these controls rests on four legal documents: (1) The 1995 *Regulations on Monitored and Controlled Chemicals* (监控化学品管理条例); (2) the 1997 *Implementation Details on the Regulations on Monitored and Controlled Chemicals* (监控化学品管理条例实施 细则); (3) the 1997 *Circular on Further Strengthening*

---

[15] This encompasses all CWC-controlled chemicals plus ten goods added in June 1998.

Figure 4.12
Government Organizations Overseeing Export Control Decisionmaking for Controlled Chemicals, 2005

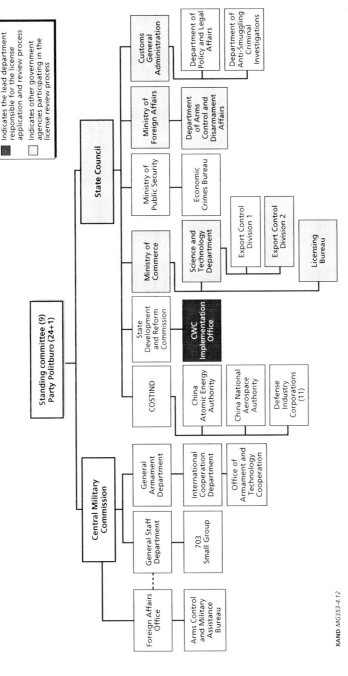

RAND *MG353-4.12*

NOTE: Controlled chemicals include all those that are CWC controlled and ten chemicals added to China's CW controls list in June 1998.

Figure 4.13
Export Control Licensing Process for Controlled Chemicals

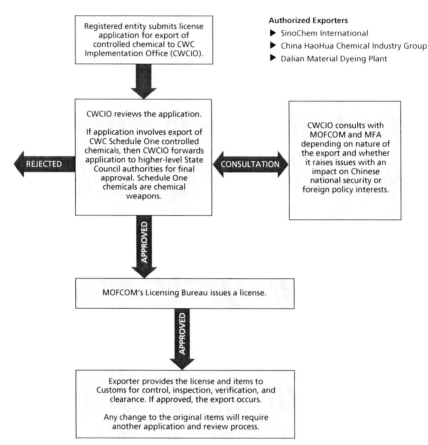

RAND MG353-4.13

NOTE: Based on 1997 Chinese *Regulations on the Export of Controlled Chemicals.* Controlled chemicals include all CWC-controlled chemicals and ten chemicals added to China's existing CW controls list in June 1998.

Figure 4.14
Government Organizations Overseeing Export Control Decisionmaking for Dual-Use Chemicals, 2005

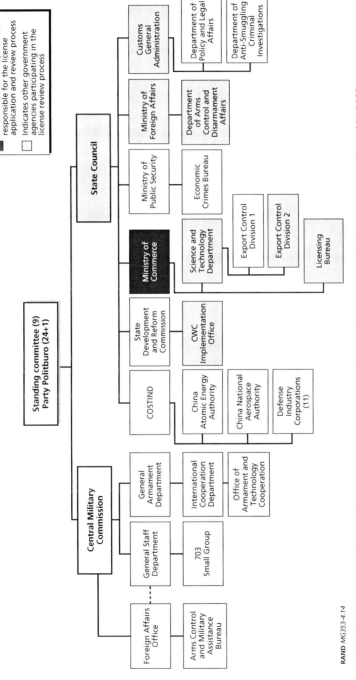

RAND MG353-4.14

NOTE: This decisionmaking applies to dual-use chemicals and related items covered in the measures adopted in 2002.

Figure 4.15
Export Control Licensing Process for Certain Chemicals and Related Equipment and Technologies

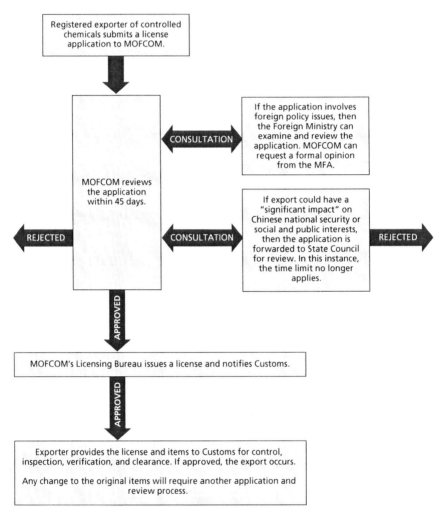

RAND *MG353-4.15*

NOTE: Based on 2002 Chinese *Measures on Export Control of Certain Chemicals and Related Equipment and Technologies.* This process applies to dual-use chemicals and related items covered in the measures adopted in 2002.

Supervision over the Import and Export of Chemical Materials That Can Be Used in the Production of Chemical Weapons; (4) the *Decree No.1 of the State Petroleum and Chemical Industry Administration: Inventory of Newly Added Varieties That Are Listed as Schedule Three Controlled Chemicals* (国家石油和化学工业局令第一号).[16]

Step 1: A registered Chinese entity[17] submits to the CWCIO a license application for the export of controlled chemicals from the CWC list or from the ten chemicals added to Chinese control lists in June 1998. The exporter must submit the standard set of required documents and certifications to complete the application. (See the requirements listed in Step Three under "Broad Outline of China's System of Controls on Sensitive Goods and Technologies.")

Step 2: CWCIO reviews the application. If the application involves the export of CWC Schedule One or Schedule Two controlled chemicals, then the CWCIO forwards the application to the State Council for final approval. In practical terms, this latter step seldom occurs. Schedule One chemicals are actual chemical weapons.

The CWCIO is more involved in reviewing license applications for CWC Schedule Three chemicals, which are dual-use chemicals. In reviewing the application, the CWCIO can consult with MOFCOM and the MFA depending on the nature of the export and whether it raises issues having an impact on Chinese national security or foreign policy interests. An intranet was established between the CWCIO and MOFCOM that allows joint review of such applications.

Step 3: If approved, MOFCOM's Licensing Bureau issues the license and notification of the approval is sent to Customs.

---

[16] This document expanded China's list of controlled chemicals to include ten chemicals from the Australian Group's control list.

[17] There are only three Chinese enterprises authorized to export controlled chemicals: Sino-Chem, China Haohua Chemical Industry Company, and Dalian Ranliao Company. It is not clear whether Sino-Chem's authorization extends to its numerous subsidiaries; if so, then that extension of authority constitutes a major weakness in China's CW controls. Dalian Ranliao is authorized to sell only one CWC Schedule Three chemical, for use in dying clothing.

Step 4: The license is given to Customs. After inspection and verification, Customs allows the export to occur. Any change to the original application will require another full review.

Tier Two: MOFCOM CW Controls[18]

The legal basis for this export control decisionmaking process resides in one document: *The 2002 Measures on Export Control of Certain Chemicals and Related Equipment and Technologies* (有关化学品及相关设备和技术出口管制办法)（and an accompanying control list known as *Certain Chemicals and Related Equipment and Technologies Export Control List* [有关化学品及相关设备和技术出口管制清单]）. These measures include a catch-all provision that allows the government to deny an export if the applicant has lied or if there is a proliferation risk—even for items not specifically on the control list.

Step 1: A registered exporter of controlled chemicals submits to MOFCOM a license application, including all relevant certifications.

Step 2: Within 45 days, MOFCOM will review the application, possibly in cooperation with CWCIO and other State Council entities.

Step 3: In cases in which the export could have a significant impact on China's "national security and social and public interests," MOFCOM, with other agencies such as the MFA, will submit the application to the State Council for review.

Step 4: If the application is approved, MOFCOM issues a license and sends a written notice to Customs.

Step 5: The license is given to Customs. After inspection and verification, Customs allows the export to occur. Any change to the original application will require another full review.

---

[18] This process covers several categories of dual-use CW-related equipment and technologies, in additional to ten dual-use chemicals.

CHAPTER FIVE

Challenges in Implementation and Enforcement of Export Controls

This chapter addresses the Chinese government's efforts to implement and enforce its export controls. Chinese implementation and enforcement of nonproliferation regulations are perhaps the most important aspects of export control administration (Figure 5.1 illustrates the government organizations involved in export control enforcement). The Chinese government's actions on these issues serve as an indicator of how great a priority it places on WMD nonproliferation. Moreover, the government's efforts in this area also offer a tangible indicator of the government's ability to live up to its nonproliferation commitments. The government's capacity to implement and enforce export controls also informs broader debates about China's capability for good governance and the implications of such governance issues for Chinese foreign policy and national security.

To date, the available data on Chinese implementation and enforcement of export controls are limited and based mainly on anecdotal accounts. The Chinese government provides very little data, such as statistics regarding license approvals or denials, to evaluate the functioning of China's export control system. These limited data suggest a mixed picture of Beijing's willingness and ability to fully enforce its WMD-related export control laws and regulations. Progress and improvements in this area continue in the face of multiple and overlapping weaknesses.

Figure 5.1
Government Organizations Involved in Export Control Enforcement and Investigations, 2005

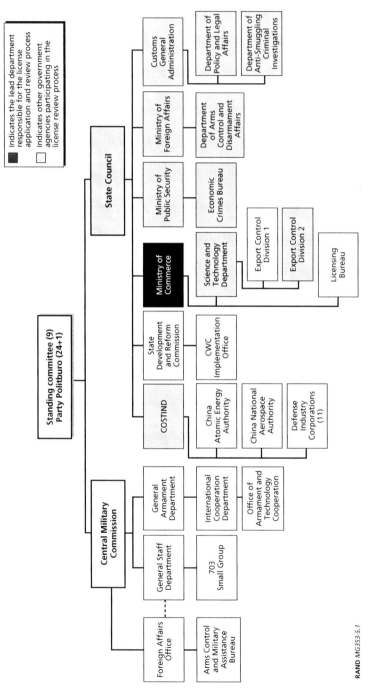

RAND *MG353-5.1*

NOTE: MOFCOM initially leads all investigations. If criminal activities are determined to be involved, MPS handles the investigation.

This study treats implementation and enforcement as distinct but related concepts. *Implementation* represents China's efforts to translate government policy into practical actions within the Chinese government and between government and industry. Implementation is related to government decisionmaking processes and the government's efforts to educate Chinese industry of its obligations under government policy. *Enforcement* is related to China's efforts to monitor the behavior of state-run entities and private companies, to identify violations by those entities and the organizations' legal obligations, and, most important, to hold these groups accountable for violating government rules. In general terms, China has made far more substantial and enduring strides toward implementation than it has toward enforcement. These issues are examined in the following sections.

Implementation

In contrast to the 1990s when implementation of WMD nonproliferation was not high on the government's agenda, the Chinese government in recent years, especially after September 11, has identified the implementation of its WMD nonproliferation commitments as a priority item. This development has been at least partially motivated by a desire to broaden nonproliferation cooperation in U.S.–China relations. Chinese leaders sought to make nonproliferation an issue of common interest with the United States rather than a source of conflict and acrimony.[1] In recent years, Beijing has sought to accomplish this shift through the institutionalization of its policy commitments into laws, regulations, and internal processes for monitoring and controlling export of sensitive WMD items. Beijing has taken a number of steps in recent years to erect a legally based export control system,

---

[1] Wang Guangya, "Keep on Improving Non-Proliferation Mechanism and Promote World Peace and Development—China's Non-Proliferation Policy and Practice," *People's Daily*, October 17, 2002, p. 1; also see Wu Xinbo, "The Promise and Limitations of Sino-US Partnership," *The Washington Quarterly*, Autumn 2004, pp. 115–126.

to set up government processes to implement the new export control structures, and to communicate how the system works to Chinese industries. This process of developing nonproliferation-related laws and regulations began in the early 1990s but has accelerated in recent years. The process is now essentially complete. Beijing has translated virtually all of its policy commitments into legally based export control regulations. These legal instruments largely reflect international standards and universally include several important features, such as an export registration and licensing system, end-user and end-use requirements, control lists, catch-all clauses, customs supervision, and, at least on paper, a system of punishment for violators.

Beyond having these laws and regulations on paper, the government has formalized a system of interagency consultation to vet license applications for WMD-related exports. Formalization of the consultation process has several elements (the major ones are outlined in Chapter Four). The government has taken other steps to bolster the operation of its export control system. For example, an intranet has been established between MOFCOM and the CWCIO to expedite review of applications for certain chemical exports. The intragovernment consultation processes have been further improved by the creation of a group of some 240 ad hoc technical experts, based in various ministries and in nongovernmental organizations (NGOs) with government ties, who can be tapped to provide technical advice on the proliferation risk of certain goods and technologies. China's December 2003 State Council–issued white paper on nonproliferation referred to these individuals as "an independent panel of technical experts."[2]

To further assist implementation of export controls, the Chinese government in 2003 developed and implemented several detailed standards used to determine whether to allow licensing of WMD-

---

[2] *China's Nonproliferation Policy and Its Measures* (*Zhongguo Bukuosan Zhengce he Cuoshi*, 中国的防扩散政策和措施*)*, Beijing, China: Information Office of the State Council, December 2003.

related exports. According to the 2003 nonproliferation white paper,[3] these standards include the following:

- Before making a decision on whether to issue an export license, the competent department will give overall consideration to the *possible effect of the relevant exports on national security and the interests of the general public, as well as [their] effect on international and regional peace and stability.* [italics added for emphasis]
- The specific factors for reference in the examination and approval process include *China's incumbent international obligations and international commitments, whether the export of the sensitive items or technologies will directly or indirectly jeopardize China's national security or public interests or constitute a potential threat, and whether [the export] conforms to the international nonproliferation situation and China's foreign policy.*
- The examination and approval department shall also make *an overall examination of the situation of the country or region where the end user is located. [The department] shall give special consideration to whether there is any risk of proliferation in the country where the end-user is located or any risk of proliferation to a third country or region, including: whether the importing country will present a potential threat to China's national security, whether it has a program for the development of WMD and their means of delivery, whether it has close trade ties with a country or region having a program for the development of WMD and their means of delivery, whether it is subject to sanctions under a UN Security Council resolution, and whether it supports terrorism or has any links with terrorist organizations.*
- Moreover, the examination and approval department shall also pay attention to *the ability of the importing country in exercising export control and whether its domestic political situation and surrounding environment are stable. The focus of examination of the*

---

[3] *China's Nonproliferation Policy and Its Measures* (*Zhongguo Bukuosan Zhengce he Cuoshi*, 中国的防扩散政策和措施*)*, 2003.

end user and end use is to judge the ability of the importing country to use the imported items or technologies, and to assess whether the importer and the end user are authentic and reliable, and whether the end use is justified.

Another key step in the government's efforts to improve implementation has been the closer and more formal integration of Chinese licensing institutions, such as MOFCOM, with Customs control. Few such linkages functioned well in the past, a situation that created many opportunities for exporters to circumvent the export control system. A computerized system now allows MOFCOM's Licensing Bureau to notify Customs when an export license has been approved; Customs can then notify MOFCOM when an item has cleared. It is not known whether this system operates in all of China's customs zones.[4]

Additional Measures: Watch Lists and End-Use/End-User Checks

Other attributes of China's export control decisionmaking processes shed light on the government's ability to implement its nonproliferation export controls. As noted above, the actual data on implementation are limited and largely based on anecdotal information. Thus, a mixed picture of the effectiveness of China's licensing system emerges. Conversations with Chinese officials indicate that China does not have a formal internal "blacklist" of foreign countries and foreign companies that are automatically barred from receiving sensitive exports. Chinese officials state that they view such a list as anathema to China's commitment to "mutual equality" in its foreign relations. However, Chinese officials have stated that they are well aware of "countries of concern" to China and treat them accordingly. Chinese officials have noted that any military-related exports to Iran, Iraq, Pakistan, Libya, and countries in Africa involved in regional conflicts are vetted very carefully. China's continued conventional military ex-

---

[4] Jonathan E. Davis, *Export Controls of the People's Republic of China 2005*, Athens, Ga.: Center for International Trade and Security, University of Georgia, February 2005, p. 41.

ports to Sudan raise questions about the utility of this informal watch list, however.

Chinese officials have stated that they have developed lists of numerous end users in various countries based on past experience, although they acknowledge the need for a more formal database. In addition, Chinese officials have said that they possess a watch list of suspect *Chinese* companies that the government monitors to prevent unlicensed exports of controlled goods.

Moreover, the government is making efforts to improve its end-use/end-user certification process, which is a major weakness at the moment. China formally established in 2003 several standards for evaluating end-use/end-user credentials:

- Bona fides of the importer, end user, and other parties involved in the transaction
- Productivity and rationality of end use
- Quantity and quality of exports
- Price of export
- Means of transportation and transportation route.

Officials from both MOFCOM and the MFA claim that they carry out end-use/end-user certification in several ways. Many of these practices are underdeveloped and, at this stage, are highly prone to manipulation and deception by either the exporter or the end user. China's most basic certification method involves reviewing documents using the standards just listed, but this method requires the ability to assess the authenticity of the information in a license application. MOFCOM and MFA can task China embassies to investigate certain end users to determine their legitimacy and the veracity of their applications. Chinese exporters are sometimes also tasked with ensuring the validity of the end-use/end-user certificates, although that involves an obvious conflict of interest. Chinese officials claim that the government of the importing nation (such as the government of Iran) is sometimes asked to verify formally the end-use/end-user certificate, and at other times the Chinese embassy of the importing nation helps to certify the end use or end user. The Chinese government, in some circumstances, will conduct end-use verification checks via its embassy in the destination country. This latter practice is far from common, however.

A more complete assessment of the functioning of China's licensing process would benefit greatly from statistics on the number of applications, approvals, and denials, and details about the frequency of PLCs and PSVs conducted by Chinese authorities. Absent such information, an assessment of China's export control system may be accurate but would be incomplete.

Government-Industry Coordination

The government has also made gradual progress in improving government-industry interactions on WMD export control. These interactions, which are critical to effective export controls, cover several dimensions, including education, outreach, and cooperation. In the past several years, government agencies have sought to educate Chinese enterprises about their export control obligations. Such education campaigns began in the mid-1990s when the government issued its first export control regulations on chemical and nuclear goods. At that time, the chemical and nuclear industries took responsibility for communicating their obligations. Both industries issued "internal circulars" (*neibu tonggao,* 内部通告) outlining new export control obligations, and some organized industry-specific seminars to educate specific enterprises. The new regulations have also appeared in industry newspapers, such as *Nuclear Industry News* (*He Gongye Bao,* 核工业报). Two of the most common means for communicating information on new regulations or newly controlled items to enterprises is via publication in the *MOFCOM Gazette* and posting the information on the MOFCOM Web site. MOFCOM also uses both these mechanisms to notify enterprises when it puts certain proliferation-sensitive items *that are not on existing control lists* under temporary government control.[5]

---

[5] Interviews with Chinese officials, Beijing, China, March 2004.

In recent years, MOFCOM has taken the lead in sponsoring export-control training programs, although the CWCIO, CAEA, COSTIND, and a few NGOs also have sponsored industry training courses. In 2000 and 2003, MOFCOM and the U.S. Commerce Department organized two U.S.-China conferences on export controls. In February 2003, MOFCOM held its first nationwide seminar on WMD export controls, which brought together officials from provincial MOFCOM bureaus. (Provincial MOFCOM officials organize meetings for local enterprises to inform those enterprises about their export control obligations.) In addition, MOFCOM officials in Beijing participate in export control meetings that are organized by CWCIO, CAEA, and COSTIND. The CWCIO staff also regularly interacts with MOFCOM to organize provincial-level seminars on China's chemical export controls, given the difficulties associated with informing China's large and growing chemical export-import industry of new rules and regulations. For example, the CWCIO held two training seminars in Fujian and Kunming in 2003 to explain changes in China's chemical export regulations. China's NGOs have also begun to assist in industrial training on export controls. In May 2004, the CACDA held a training session on WMD controls for Chinese Customs officials in the seaport city of Dalian; CACDA also sponsored other seminars in Beijing.

Beyond such education measures, the government has leveraged the Internet to improve government-industry coordination on WMD export controls. MOFCOM in 2004 established two very detailed and comprehensive Web sites to facilitate the registration and application processes related to its WMD export-control licensing system. Pages from those Web sites are shown in Figure 5.2a and Figure 5.2b.

The site shown in Figure 5.2b is professionally created and separate from the general MOFCOM Web site; it was specifically designed to manage the entire export registration and license application process. (See Figure 3.1 in Chapter Three.)

**Figure 5.2a: Chinese Export Control Web Site
(http://exportcontrol.mofcom.gov.cn/)**

These Web sites include sections on laws and regulations, control lists, the end-use/end-user certification process, frequently asked questions about the licensing process, and reports on new rules and regulations. Perhaps most important, all the application forms related to registration (of an exporter of sensitive commodities), the license applications, and the end-user certificates can be downloaded from these Web sites. The Chinese have also created separate documents detailing all of the specific responsibilities of Chinese exporters of sensitive commodities. MOFCOM is in the process of establishing a system by which license applications can be submitted online as well by mail. For Chinese enterprises, the entire registration and licensing processes soon can be done completely online.

**Figure 5.2b: Chinese Export Control Web Site
(http://exctrl.ec.com.cn/tecp/corp_index.jsp)**

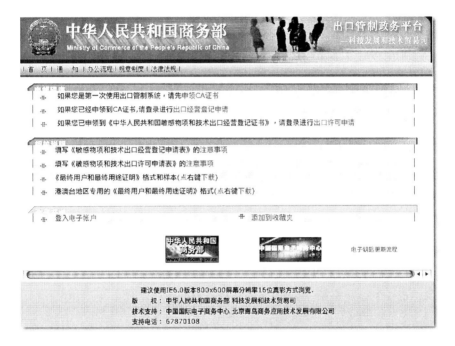

As a further indication of China's efforts to improve its implementation of existing controls, MOFCOM has reached out to academic research centers for advice and counsel on WMD nonproliferation issues. MOFCOM has approached nonproliferation specialists at Fudan University, Qinghua University, and CASS for advice on erecting an effective export control system. The nongovernment specialists at these centers have, in return, shared the fruits of their research with MOFCOM officials in order to improve China's efforts to fulfill its nonproliferation commitments. Both Qinghua and Fudan Universities, drawing on their existing expertise on arms control and nonproliferation issues, have explored the possibility of establishing small nonproliferation export control research programs.

Enterprise-Level Controls

Beyond improvements in government-industry interactions, some data indicate that there have also been improvements in enterprise-level controls on sensitive exports (i.e., industry compliance). Beginning in 2002, some major state-owned firms began paying much more attention to their internal controls on sensitive exports. Interviews with industry officials from a large state-owned firm indicated that such changes are taking place.[6] For example, one company set up a small export-control research bureau within its Systems Research Institute. The goal of this bureau is to research the role of industry in U.S. export control decisionmaking and provide suggestions for promoting the company's efforts to improve internal compliance. One industry official highlighted several steps his company had taken to improve internal monitoring of exports. Those steps included a system for auditing all export contracts; the participation of technical experts in contract audits; development of internal software for managing the auditing process; interaction with Chinese NGOs (such as CACDA) on dangerous end users; development of procedures to manage exports of noncontrolled items; training of all regional and local managers, not just senior managers who reside in Beijing; export control training for all new employees; and establishment of a dedicated export-control department. It is not clear whether any of these measures has been implemented by a wide range of Chinese firms, especially firms that long have been involved in exporting sensitive goods.

Another major step toward implementation of export controls has been the establishment of a harmonized system (HS) of Customs codes. In the past two years, China has developed a system of eight-digit codes that apply to many categories of exports, including some sensitive WMD-related items. The purpose of this system is to facilitate the Customs inspection and clearance process. The existence of a specific commodity code on an export tells the Customs officer whether an export license is required. Theoretically, this system al-

---

[6] Interviews with Chinese officials, Beijing, China, April 2004.

lows effective controls to be carried out, regardless of the degree of training or knowledge of the Customs officers.

As of summer 2004, about 35 percent of China's controlled goods and technologies had been assigned HS numbers. One limitation of this system is its reliance on eight-digit codes, which are non-specific in some instances. For example, some eight-digit codes include types of high-tech goods that do not require an export license. A recent indicator of how well the system is functioning is the interaction between foreign companies in China and MOFCOM. Since the establishment of the HS system, some foreign companies have had to apply to MOFCOM for an export license even though the export is not on a designated control list; this situation occurs when an item falls into a broad HS category that includes both controlled and uncontrolled items. To address this problem, Chinese officials are considering moving to a 10- or 12-digit system, which would allow them to specifically match HS codes with control lists of sensitive goods.

Implementation Weaknesses and Limitations

The Chinese government faces numerous limitations in its ability to manage various export control processes. The main weaknesses are a shortage of qualified people for license review, inadequate management, and insufficient financial and technical resources. The Second Division of MOFCOM's Science and Technology Department, which is devoted to export control issues, is staffed by only eight to ten people. Most are under the age of 40, and some are recent university graduates. Most of the staff, except for the division's leadership, possess minimal experience with and interest in working on export control issues. Also, there appears to be minimal support within MOFCOM at the department level and higher for a greater priority being placed on nonproliferation export controls. In essence, more and better-trained officials are needed to handle the growing demands of export control licensing and compliance. Furthermore, China's Customs administration has come to realize the importance of the nonproliferation issue only recently, and, as a result, it lacks exposure to and expertise on WMD export controls. Customs officials are currently receiving training in this area. Many Customs border posts also lack the equipment to conduct effective inspections. For example, Customs inspection stations in Dandong, on China's border with North Korea, lack X-ray machines to scan vehicles and thus need to rely on manual checks, which are time consuming and far less effective. In addition, the small area available at Dandong to conduct such checks further inhibits adequate inspections.[7]

Going beyond the personnel issues, MOFCOM as of 2004 lacked a computerized database of past and current export licenses (applied, denied, or approved) and of end users and end uses in various countries. The MFA also lacks such a critical resource, or links to one. These shortfalls dramatically limit the government's ability to verify end users or end uses—leaving a gap in the compliance system. MOFCOM officials stated in late 2004 that such a computerized database is only now being created, and it will take some time to build it.

A final issue is the degree to which MOFCOM's Second Division possesses incentives to address export control issues. On the one hand, there are significant political incentives for greater export control compliance, given the priority that China's senior leaders have placed on nonproliferation compliance. Yet, it is not clear that MOFCOM's senior officials share this goal, given the fact that their organization is supposed to promote international trade, not limit it. In addition, in 2004, the Chinese leadership began promoting a business strategy called the "go-out" (*zou chu*, 走出) strategy to help Chinese enterprises globalize their businesses and become more profitable. Export controls may not be immediately welcomed in such an environment, both within MOFCOM and outside of it. In addition, MOFCOM officials have inquired at international meetings about how they can make money via export control administration, suggesting the existence of some type of internal requirement for each division to generate funds. It is not clear if the Science and Technology Department's Second Division is obligated to meet this requirement.

---

[7] Davis, 2005, p. 43.

Enforcement

China's enforcement of its export control regulations is the weakest link in its export control system. The government's ability to detect, catch, investigate, and penalize export control violators is substantially underdeveloped. Critical gaps exist in many aspects of export control enforcement, especially in monitoring, interdiction, and penalization. To be sure, these capabilities are better than they were a few years ago, but much more work needs to be done.

A major problem in enforcement is that China currently appears to rely largely on the provision of intelligence information from foreign governments to find out about pending exports of illicit WMD-related goods and technologies. Many Chinese interdictions to date have relied on intelligence data from the United States, the UK, and perhaps Israel. It is not known whether China has initiated investigations based on data obtained from Chinese agencies, although such actions are likely. China is trying to build up a capability within its Ministry of State Security (MSS, *Guojia Anquan Bu*, 国家 安全部) to monitor foreigners and front companies operating in China that are seeking to procure controlled WMD-related goods. An interesting insight into the dark subject of MSS surveillance in China appeared in a Western news article about China's relationship with Pakistani nuclear scientist A. Q. Kahn. The news report quoted a Pakistani diplomat being told by a Chinese counterpart that Kahn was in China bribing Chinese nuclear industry officials to sell him controlled nuclear goods; Beijing wanted Pakistan's government to make Kahn leave China.[8]

After the Chinese government receives intelligence data about a pending export of controlled goods, it often launches an investigation to determine if an authorized export will occur. In the past, the MFA

---

[8] As quoted from the news article, "On a trip to Beijing, one senior Pakistani diplomat said, Chinese authorities 'took me aside, said they knew it would be embarrassing, but A. Q. Khan was in China and bribing people, and they wanted him out.' The diplomat said Pakistan confiscated a false passport, but Khan kept traveling." See Barton Gellman and Dafna Linzer, "Unprecedented Peril Forces Tough Calls, President Faces a Multi-Front Battle Against Threats Known, Unknown," *The Washington Post,* October 26, 2004, p. A01.

conducted the investigation, usually in cooperation with provincial officials. Currently, MOFCOM takes charge of the investigation. It has lead authority on all export control investigations, a new power for MOFCOM. In most investigations, MOFCOM works with MFA, Customs, the Port Authority, provincial MOFCOM officials, and sometimes the MPS. Because intelligence data sometimes require an immediate response (e.g., when an illicit shipment is about to occur), the Chinese government has established a rapid-response task force. This task force was created in the wake of a 2003 event in which China interdicted a shipment of TBP headed for North Korea. According to Chinese officials, the members of the task force include officials from MOFCOM, MFA, COSTIND, Customs, and the MPS.[9]

The goal of these and other investigations is to determine if an export control violation has, in fact, occurred and why it occurred. In other words, was it the result of ignorance or willful deception by the exporter? If the infraction is the result of ignorance on the part of the enterprise or mistakes by the company during the licensing process, then MOFCOM can levy (and has levied) administrative sanctions. These sanctions carry penalties ranging from monetary fines to suspension of export-import privileges; they can include a full revocation of a business license. The legal basis for these fines is outlined in various export control regulations, China's Criminal Law, and the 1996 Law on Administrative Punishments. MOFCOM officials say they have already imposed administrative sanctions (*xingzheng chufa*, 行政处罚) on several Chinese companies, including the suspension of one firm's business license. On May 25, 2004, MOFCOM—for the first time ever—published on its Web site notice of the penalization of two entities: a trading company from Jiangsu province and a chemical producer from Shandong province. Both firms were fined millions of *renminbi* (thousands of U.S. dollars) for exporting without proper authorization items covered in China's 2002 regulations on

---

[9] Interviews with Chinese officials, Beijing, China, 2003 and 2004.

dual-use missile goods and technologies.[10] If MOFCOM determines that *criminal* activity has occurred, it refers the case to the MPS for a criminal investigation. The MPS recently established a unit within its Economic Crimes Division to conduct export control investigations. Although the precise triggers for a criminal investigation are not yet clear, they may involve falsifying documents and lying to Chinese officials. MOFCOM is also exploring the establishment of two legal standards—intent and the financial value of goods—to determine whether to initiate a criminal investigation versus just applying administrative penalties. MOFCOM officials have stated that there are currently two such cases under criminal investigation, but neither one has been concluded. There is no indication of whether or when they will be forwarded to the Procuracy.

Continuing weaknesses in China's ability to investigate export control violations include MOFCOM and MPS's lack of experience in this area. In particular, their attitude in approaching such investigations creates a weakness in their investigative capabilities. First, MOFCOM and MPS's approach has been reactive, relying on the provision of Western intelligence data. Second, there is a lack of the healthy skepticism about Chinese firms that is needed to effectively conduct such investigations. MOFCOM officials are too willing to accept explanations from company officials about end uses and end users without pushing them for further information or questioning the veracity of their explanations. Increased interactions with Western export-control enforcement agencies involved in investigations may help to alleviate these problems.

In addition, it is not clear whether MOFCOM officials have sufficient political backing and authority to conduct investigations of large and politically influential state-owned enterprises, such as NORINCO or New Era/*Xinshidai*. Such large corporations in some

---

[10] "Two Chinese Companies Fined for Violating Regulations on Missile Export Control," *People's Daily Online,* last updated May 26, 2004 (http://exportcontrol.mofcom.gov.cn/article/200408/20040800269548_1.xml, in Chinese; http://english.peopledaily.com.cn/200405/26/eng20040526_144379.html, in English; last accessed April 18, 2005).

instances can possess the same status as government ministries, which significantly complicates MOFCOM's ability to request access to those corporations' export records or to question the judgment of their leadership on exports of sensitive goods and technologies. In the past, the United States has publicly questioned the export activities of major state-owned enterprises in order to galvanize China's leadership to investigate the export practices of those companies. Given the importance of industry self-compliance to the effective functioning of China's export control system, the export practices of China's large, state-owned, and politically influential enterprises will need to be addressed before China's export control system can move to the next stage of development.

CHAPTER SIX

Future Challenges for China's Export Control System

China's export controls on sensitive goods and technologies have come a long way since the first regulations on exports of such items were adopted in the mid-1990s. Yet, the export control system still has a long way to go to reach the level of a fully functioning system that regularly monitors and polices the activities of exporters involved in selling WMD-related goods and technologies. The system currently faces several challenges in achieving this goal; in the future, new challenges will further tax the current system. Those new challenges include the following:

- **Regularizing Implementation.** Improving the government's ability to implement and enforce existing rules and regulations is a key challenge. A top priority in this area should include establishing a computer database to track licenses (approved and denied). This database will improve the government's ability to verify end-use and end-user data. A continuing implementation challenge involves educating Chinese enterprises about their export control obligations, with self-compliance as a long-term goal. The Chinese government also needs to establish a neutral and effective end-use/end-user verification system that is not limited to certification by the exporter and/or the importer's government. China will also need to target resources toward developing a system of pre-license checks and post-shipment verification.

- **Boosting Enforcement.** The challenges for export control enforcement are even greater than those related to implementation. China needs to erect an effective mechanism to identify unlicensed exports and prevent them from occurring. For this process, China is currently largely reliant on the information provided by foreign governments. Beijing also needs to improve and provide more authority for the export-control investigation process among government agencies, especially the process related to criminal investigations. Much more personnel training and resources need to be devoted to enforcement of export controls.
- **Motivating Self-Compliance by Enterprises.** A challenge related to implementation and enforcement is incentivizing Chinese companies to comply with national export-control regulations. Incentivizing has not occurred on a wide scale and is a critical element of effective policymaking on WMD nonproliferation. It is not clear whether Chinese companies currently see the high costs from penalties associated with noncompliance. The Chinese government must demonstrate to enterprises that there are stiff penalties for violating export control regulations. Administrative penalties have been levied against some companies, but only in limited ways. Chinese officials have said that criminal investigations related to export control violations are occurring, but no criminal penalties have been issued yet.[1] The Chinese government will need to publicize a high-profile case with severe penalties to demonstrate to Chinese firms the costs of noncompliance with WMD export control regulations.
- **Government Reorganization.** The Chinese bureaucracy has been downsizing and reorganizing significantly in recent years. Government departments have been abolished, renamed, and reorganized numerous times in the past decade as part of China's ongoing economic reform effort. These organizational changes have complicated export control administration due to

---

[1] Interviews with Chinese officials, Beijing, China, March 2004.

the elimination, renaming, and/or reconstitution of government organizations that were part of the licensing process. Such bureaucratic reshuffling will likely continue in the future. Chinese officials need to continue to adapt their decisionmaking processes to account for the changing size and shape of the government bureaucracy.

- **The WTO Multiplier Effect.** Now that China is a member of the WTO, the number of entities in China with authority to import and export goods will increase exponentially. This growth has already begun. The process of getting a business license in China is being merged with the process of getting import-export authorization. As the number of trading entities increases, the task of export-control education and enforcement will grow accordingly. The Chinese government will need to devote even greater resources to informing exporters about their export control obligations. Under these changing conditions, the importance of motivating enterprises to abide by their obligations (i.e., self-compliance) will become even more critical than before.

- **Enterprise Privatization.** The number of nonstate private enterprises in China has increased as a result of the broad economic reform project begun in the early 1980s. Related to this privatization trend is the shutting down of small- and medium-sized state-owned enterprises (SOEs), which are a drain on government resources. As these SOEs have closed, their personnel have set up private enterprises involved in the trade of goods and services related to their former SOEs. Some of China's defense enterprises and other critical industries are currently experiencing this transition, which has resulted in the growth of small, private entrepreneurs willing to trade in sensitive goods and technologies such as controlled dual-use nuclear or chemical items. The proliferation of these small, mom-and-pop boutique firms (especially in the chemical industry) will increase the burden on the Chinese government to effectively vet exports of sensitive goods and technologies and prevent illicit transfers.

- **Growing Foreign Penetration of China's Economy.** As China's economy continues to open up to foreign involvement, especially under the WTO, foreign enterprises will have far more opportunities to become involved in sectors of Chinese industry that were once taboo. As the depth and breadth of foreign business activities in China grow, the opportunities for foreign procurement agents and front companies to set up shop in China will also increase. Some foreign agents and enterprises already operate in China, and they have taken advantage of China's weak regulatory environment to illicitly procure controlled items for their national WMD-related development programs. The Chinese government will need to devote far more resources to prevent the exploitation of its growing economic openness by foreign agents who are seeking access to sensitive goods and technologies.

Application for Registration as an Authorized Exporter of Sensitive Goods and Technology

中华人民共和国敏感物项和技术出口经营登记申请表

警告：根据《中华人民共和国核两用品及相关技术出口管制条例》、《中华人民共和国导弹及相关物项和技术出口管制条例》、《中华人民共和国生物两用品及相关设备和技术出口管制条例》和《有关化学品及相关设备和技术出口管制办法》的规定，经营者必须如实填写下表。任何以隐瞒实情、提供虚假陈述或其他不正当方式骗取登记的，都将依法受到严格处罚。

企业名称	中文	
	英文	
企业住所		
企业类型	营业执照注册号	
成立日期	法定代表人	
注册资本	进出口企业代码	
电话	传真	
电子邮箱	联系人	
分支机构		
经营类别	□核两用品及相关技术　　□生物两用品及相关设备和技术 □化学品及相关设备和技术　　□导弹相关物项和技术　　□其他敏感物项和技术	
申请经营的物项和技术的主要内容（可另附页）		
申请类型	□首次登记　　　□换领　　　□补办	

注：本表一式两联，须一并使用，并骑缝加盖企业印章。

申请理由				
其他情况	1. 是否了解国家有关出口管制的法律法规？		□是	□否
	2. 是否经营过所申请经营物项和技术的出口？		□是	□否
	3. 是否了解所申请经营物项和技术的性能或指标？		□是	□否
	4. 是否了解所申请经营物项和技术的主要用途？		□是	□否
	5. 是否有专人负责出口的管理和跟踪服务？		□是	□否
	6. 是否曾经受过刑事处罚和行政处罚？如有，请列举。		□是	□否

兹保证已如实填写上述内容，并将在今后经营活动中严格遵守国家有关出口管制法律、法规和规章的规定。

法定代表人签字（加盖公章）

年　　　月　　　日

以下由主管部门填写

审核意见

经办：　　　　　复核：　　　　批准：

受理日期	年　　月　　日	备注：
登记证号		
发证日期	年　　月　　日	

商务部监制（2003-B）

Application for a License to Export Sensitive Goods and Technology

中华人民共和国敏感物项和技术出口许可申请表

申请编号：

申请类别	商品分类	进口国（地区）
出口商		出口物项
出口经营登记证号		收货人
进出口企业代码		最终用户
合同号		贸易方式
合同签订日期		报关口岸
付款方式		运输方式

商品情况

序号	商品名称	海关编码	数量	单位	单价	总值	总值折美元
商品技术描述（请对照管制清单，可另加附页）					总计		

商品主要用途（可另加附页）

本合同项下商品的最终用途

注：1. 本表一式两联，须一并使用，并骑缝加盖企业印章。
　　2. 申请编号由审批机关统一编写。

进口商、最终用户及国内生产商情况		
进口商名称、地址（外文名称及中文译名）		
联系人	电话/传真	
最终用户名称、地址（外文名称及中文译名）		
联系人	电话/传真	
进口商和最终用户的详细情况（可另加附页）		
国内生产商名称、地址		
联系人	电话/传真	
出口商情况		
名称（中英名称）　　　　　　　地址		
主要负责人　　　　　经办人　　　　　邮编		
电话/传真　　　　　　　　电子邮件		

其他情况	1. 是否了解国家相关出口管制条例（办法）及其所附"出口管制清单"内容？	☐是	☐否
	2. 是否了解所申请出口产品和技术的性能或指标？	☐是	☐否
	3. 是否了解所申请出口产品和技术的主要用途？	☐是	☐否
	4. 是否经营过所申请出口产品和技术的出口？	☐是	☐否
	5. 是否有专人或专门机构负责出口管制产品和技术的出口管理？	☐是	☐否
	6. 是否了解进口商和最终用户的情况？	☐是	☐否
	7. 是否曾与进口商有过商业往来？	☐是	☐否

　　兹保证已如实填写上述内容，并将在出口经营活动中严格遵守国家有关出口管制法律、法规和规章的规定。

法定代表人签字（加盖公章）

年　　　　月

日

商务部监制（2003-B）

End-User and End-Use Certificates

英文格式:

End-User Certificate

_____(Date)

Ministry of Commerce of P. R. China,

We, _____(Company name and address), are the end-user of (Commodity name) purchased from the Chinese company (Company name) under contract_____(Contract No.). We guarantee that we will not transfer the above-said _____ (Commodity name) to any third party without the consent of the Chinese government.

We, _____(company name), will only use the (Commodity name) purchased from Chinese company _____(Company name) under contract_____(Contract No.) for/in_____(End-use). We guarantee that we will not use the above-said _____ (Commodity name) in the storing, processing, producing and treating of weapons of mass destruction and their delivery systems or any use other than we declared above.

Signature/Company Stamp

_____(Name in print)

_____(Title)

_____(Company name)

中文译本格式：

最终用户和最终用途证明

中华人民共和国商务部：

我们，＿＿（公司名称、地址），是从中国＿＿＿＿＿（公司名称）购买的＿＿（合同号）项下的＿＿＿＿＿（商品名称）的最终用户。未经中国政府许可，我们不将上述＿＿＿＿＿（商品名称）转让给任何第三方。

我们，＿＿（公司名称），将把从中国＿＿＿＿＿（公司名称）购买的＿＿（合同号）项下的＿＿＿＿＿（商品名称）用于＿＿＿＿＿（最终用途）。未经中国政府许可，我们不将上述＿＿＿＿＿（商品名称）用于储存、加工、生产、处理大规模杀伤性武器及其运载系统以及申明以外的其他用途。

＿＿＿＿＿＿＿＿＿＿（最终用户公司名称）

＿＿＿＿＿＿＿＿＿（签字人职务）

＿＿＿＿＿＿＿＿＿（印刷体签字人姓名）

＿＿＿＿＿＿（出口商企业印章）　　　年　　月　　日

样　　本

英文原件：

End-Use Certificate

May 15, 2003

Ministry of Commerce of P. R. China,

We, ABC Company (1, A Street, UK), are the end-user of titanium powder purchased from the Chinese company DEF LTD under contract No. S/C200301. We guarantee that we will not transfer the above-said titanium powder to any third party without the consent of the Chinese government.

We, ABC Company, will only use the titanium powder purchased from the Chinese company DEF LTD under contract No. S/C200301 in metal coating. We guarantee that we will not use the above-said titanium powder in the storing, processing, producing and treating of weapons of mass destruction and their delivery systems or any use other than we declared above.

Signature/Stamp
Anderson Campbell
General Manager
ABC Company

中文译文：

最终用户和最终用途证明

中华人民共和国商务部：

我们，ABC 公司（英国 A 大街 1 号），是从中国 DEF 公司购买的 S/C200301 合同项下的钛粉的最终用户。未经中国政府同意，我们不将上述钛粉转让给任何第三方。

我们，ABC 公司，将把从中国 DEF 公司购买的 S/C200301 合同项下的钛粉用于金属喷涂方面。未经中国政府同意，我们不将上述钛粉用于储存、加工、生产、处理大规模杀伤性武器及其运载系统以及申明以外的其他用途。

ABC 公司

总经理

安德森·坎贝尔

2003 年 5 月 15 日

注：中文译本需加盖出口商企业印章

End-User Certificate for Hong Kong, Taiwan, and Macao

最终用户和最终用途证明

（仅供香港、澳门、台湾地区最终用户使用）

中华人民共和国商务部：

　　我公司，_____（公司中、英文全名，注册地址），是从中国大陆____（出口商名称）购买的_____（合同号）合同项下的____（商品名称）的最终用户。我公司保证，未经中华人民共和国商务部许可，不将上述物项转让给任何第三方。

　　我公司，_____（公司中、英文全名，注册地址），将把从中国大陆____（出口商名称）购买的_____（合同号）合同项下的_____（商品名称）用于____（最终用途）。我公司保证不将上述_____（商品名称）用于生产、加工、储存、处理大规模杀伤性武器及其运载系统以及上述申明以外的其他用途。

　　　　　　　　　　_____（最终用户公司名称）

　　　　　　　　　　_____（签字人职务）

　　　　　　　　　　　　签字/公司印章

　　　　　　　　　　_____（印刷体签字人全名）

　　　　　　　　年　　月　　日

Bibliography

Bhatia, Shyman, *Nuclear Rivals in the Middle East*, New York, N.Y.: Routledge Press, 1988.

China's Non-Proliferation Policy and Measures, (*Zhongguo Bukuosan Zhengce He Cuoshi*, 中国的防扩散政策和措施), Beijing, China: State Council Information Office, December 2003 (http://www.china.org.cn/e-white/20031202/index.htm; last accessed April 2004).

Cupitt, Richard T., and Yuzo Murayama, *Export Controls in the People's Republic of China, Status Report 1998*, Athens, Ga.: Center for International Trade and Security, University of Georgia, 1998.

Davis, Jonathan E., *Export Controls of the People's Republic of China 2005*, Athens, Ga.: Center for International Trade and Security, University of Georgia, February 2005.

Davis, Zachary S., "China's Nonproliferation and Export Control Policies: Boom or Bust for the NPT Regime?" *Asian Survey*, June 1995, pp. 587–603.

"Fact Sheet: China's Nuclear and Related Dual-Use Export Controls," U.S. Department of State, International Information Programs, issued with the testimony of Deputy Assistant Secretary of State for Nonproliferation Robert J. Einhorn before the House Committee on International Relations, February 4, 1998 (http://www.usconsulate.org.hk/uscn/state/1998/0204b.htm; last accessed April 2005).

Frieman, Wendy, *China, Arms Control, and Nonproliferation*, London, UK: Routledge Curzon, May 2004.

Fu Cong, "An Introduction of China's Export Control System," Department of Arms Control and Disarmament, Ministry of Foreign Affairs of

China, statement at Workshop on Nonproliferation Export Control Regimes, Tokyo, December 11–12, 1997.

Gelb, Leslie, "Peking Said to Balk at Nuclear Pledges," *New York Times*, June 23, 1984, p. 3.

Gellman, Barton, and Dafna Linzer, "Unprecedented Peril Forces Tough Calls, President Faces a Multi-Front Battle Against Threats Known, Unknown," *The Washington Post,* October 26, 2004, p. A01.

Gill, Bates, and Evan S. Medeiros, "The Foreign and Domestic Influences on China Arms Control and Nonproliferation Policies," *China Quarterly*, Vol. 161, No. 1, pp. 66–94.

Heikal, Mohamed, *The Cairo Documents*, New York, N.Y.: Doubleday Press, 1973.

Lardy, Nicholas R., *Foreign Trade and Economic Reform in China, 1978–1990*, Cambridge, UK: Cambridge University Press, 1992.

Lewis, John Wilson, and Hua Di, "China's Ballistic Missile Programs: Technologies, Strategies, and Goals," *International Security*, Fall 1992.

Li Bin, "Comments on the Chinese Regulation on Missile Technology Export Control," Qinghua University, August 26, 2002 (http://learn.tsinghua.edu.cn/homepage/2000990313/eexctl.htm; last accessed May 2, 2005).

Lu Ning, *The Dynamics of Foreign-Policy Decisionmaking in China*, Boulder, Colo.: Westview Press, 1997.

Medeiros, Evan S., "China, WMD Proliferation, and the 'China Threat' Debate," *Issues & Studies,* Vol. 366, No. 1, January/February 2000, pp. 19–48.

Medeiros, Evan S., "Rebuilding Bilateral Consensus: Assessing U.S.-China Arms Control and Nonproliferation Achievements," *The Nonproliferation Review,* Vol. 8, No. 1, Spring 2001, pp. 131–140.

Medeiros, Evan S., and Bates Gill, *Chinese Arms Exports: Policy, Players, and Process*, Carlisle, Pa.: Strategic Studies Institute, U.S. Army War College, 2000.

Mulvenon, James C., *Chinese Military Commerce and U.S. National Security*, Santa Monica, Calif.: RAND Corporation, MR-907.0-CAPP, 1997.

Naughton, Barry, *Growing Out of the Plan*, Cambridge, UK: Cambridge University Press, 1996.

Norris, Robert S. et al., *Chinese, French, and British Nuclear Weapons, Nuclear Weapons Databook*, Vol. 5, Washington, D.C.: Natural Resources Defense Council, 1995.

"The Pakistani Nuclear Program," June 23, 1983, U.S. Department of State, Bureau of Intelligence and Research, declassified and released under the Freedom of Information Act to the National Security Archive, Washington, D.C., January 17, 1991.

"Remarks at Conference on China-U.S. Relations," Secretary of State Colin L. Powell, Texas A&M University, College Station, Texas, November 5, 2003 (U.S. Department of State Web site, http://www.state.gov/secretary/former/powell/remarks/2003/25950.htm; last accessed April 12, 2005).

Shichor, Yitzhak, *East Wind over Arabia: Origins and Implications of the Sino-Saudi Missile Deal, China Research Monographs*, No. 35, Berkeley, Calif.: Institute of Asian Studies, Center for Chinese Studies, University of California, 1989.

Shichor, Yitzhak, "Israel's Military Transfers to China and Taiwan," *Survival*, Spring 1998, pp. 69–91.

Shichor, Yitzhak, "Peaceful Fallout: The Conversion of China's Military-Nuclear Complex to Civilian Use," Brief 10, Bonn, Germany: Bonn International Center for Conversion, November 1997.

Spector, Leonard S., *Nuclear Proliferation Today*, New York, N.Y.: Vintage Books, 1984.

"Two Chinese Companies Fined for Violating Regulations on Missile Export Control," *People's Daily Online,* last updated May 26, 2004 (http://exportcontrol.mofcom.gov.cn/article/200408/20040800269548_1.xml, in Chinese; http://english.peopledaily.com.cn/200405/26/eng20040526_144379.html, in English; last accessed April 18, 2005).

Wang Guangya, "Keep on Improving Non-Proliferation Mechanism and Promote World Peace and Development—China's Non-Proliferation Policy and Practice," *People's Daily*, October 17, 2002.

Warrick, Joy, "Albania's Chemical Cache Raises Fears About Others, Long-Forgotten Arms Had Little or No Security," *Washington Post*, January 10, 2005.

Weixing Hu, "China's Nuclear Export Controls: Policy and Regulations," *The Nonproliferation Review*, Vol. 1, No. 2, Winter 1994.

"Will China Assume a New Responsibility?" *Washington Post*, November 22, 1971.

Wright, David, *Assessment of the North Korean Missile Threat*, Cambridge, Mass.: Union of Concerned Scientists (www.ucsusa.org), February 2003.

Wu Xinbo, "The Promise and Limitations of Sino-US Partnership," *The Washington Quarterly*, Autumn 2004.

Yuan Jing-dong, Phillip P. Saunders, and Stephanie Lieggi, "Recent Developments in China's Export Controls: New Regulations and New Challenges," *The Nonproliferation Review*, Vol. 9, No 3, Fall/Winter 2003, pp. 153–167.